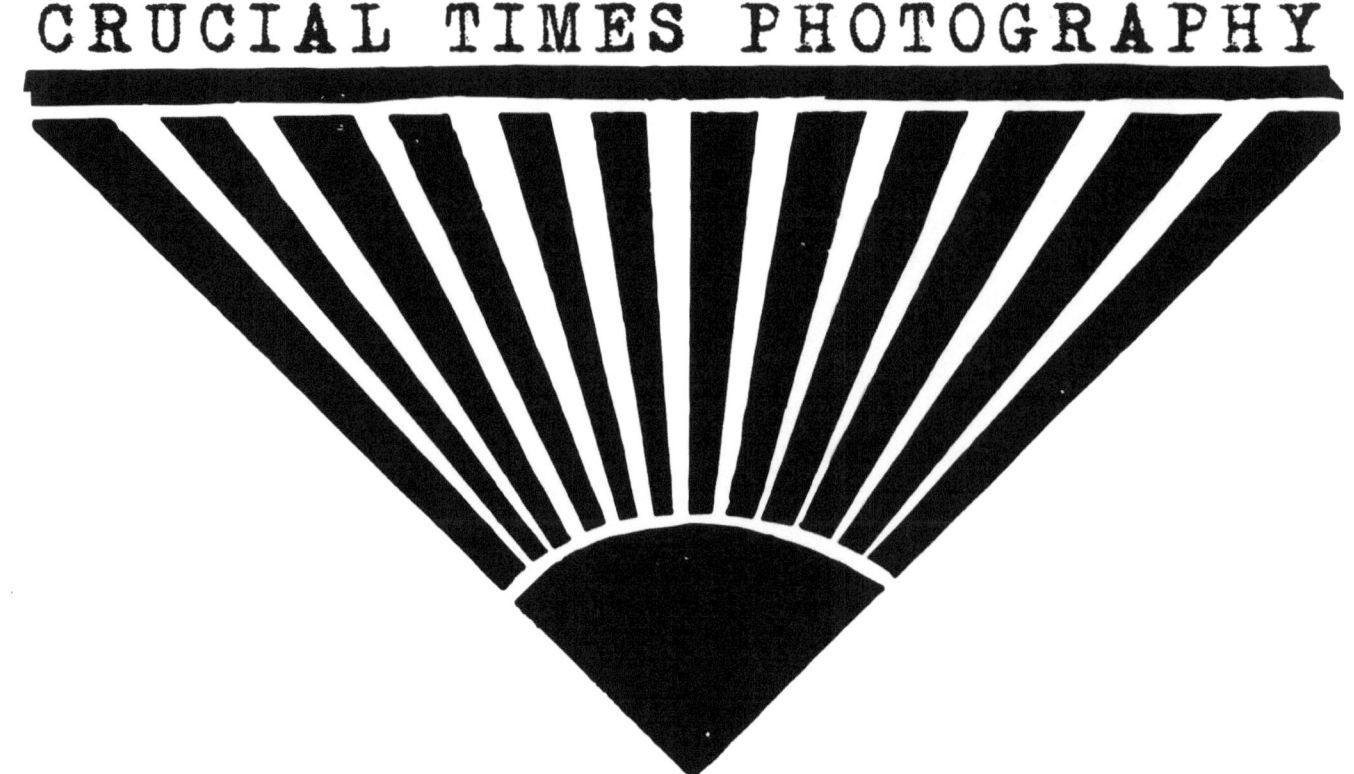

The Crucial Times Collective is a small group of photographers documenting what we find meaningful, unusual, emotional, inspiring, bold, beautiful, mysterious, powerful, and intriguing. We are unafraid of and drawn to the subversive and transgressive. While our individual creative styles may be unique, we collaborate to share our images via exhibition and print. Thank you for taking a look through our lens.

PHOTOGRAPHERS

Bryan Hannah

Khari Cowell

Michelle Camy

Miles Claibourn

Sean Mellon

John Simcox

Travis California

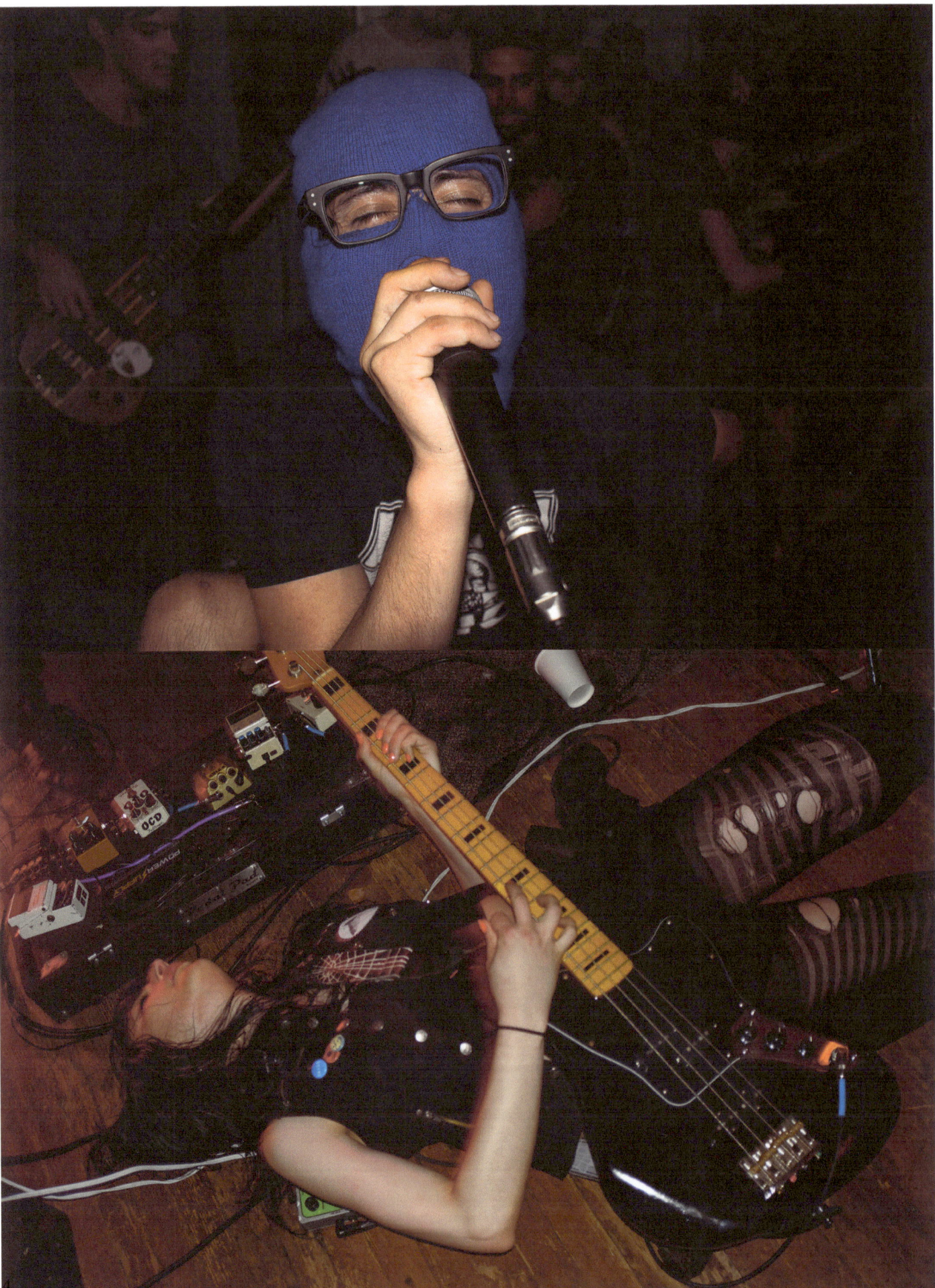

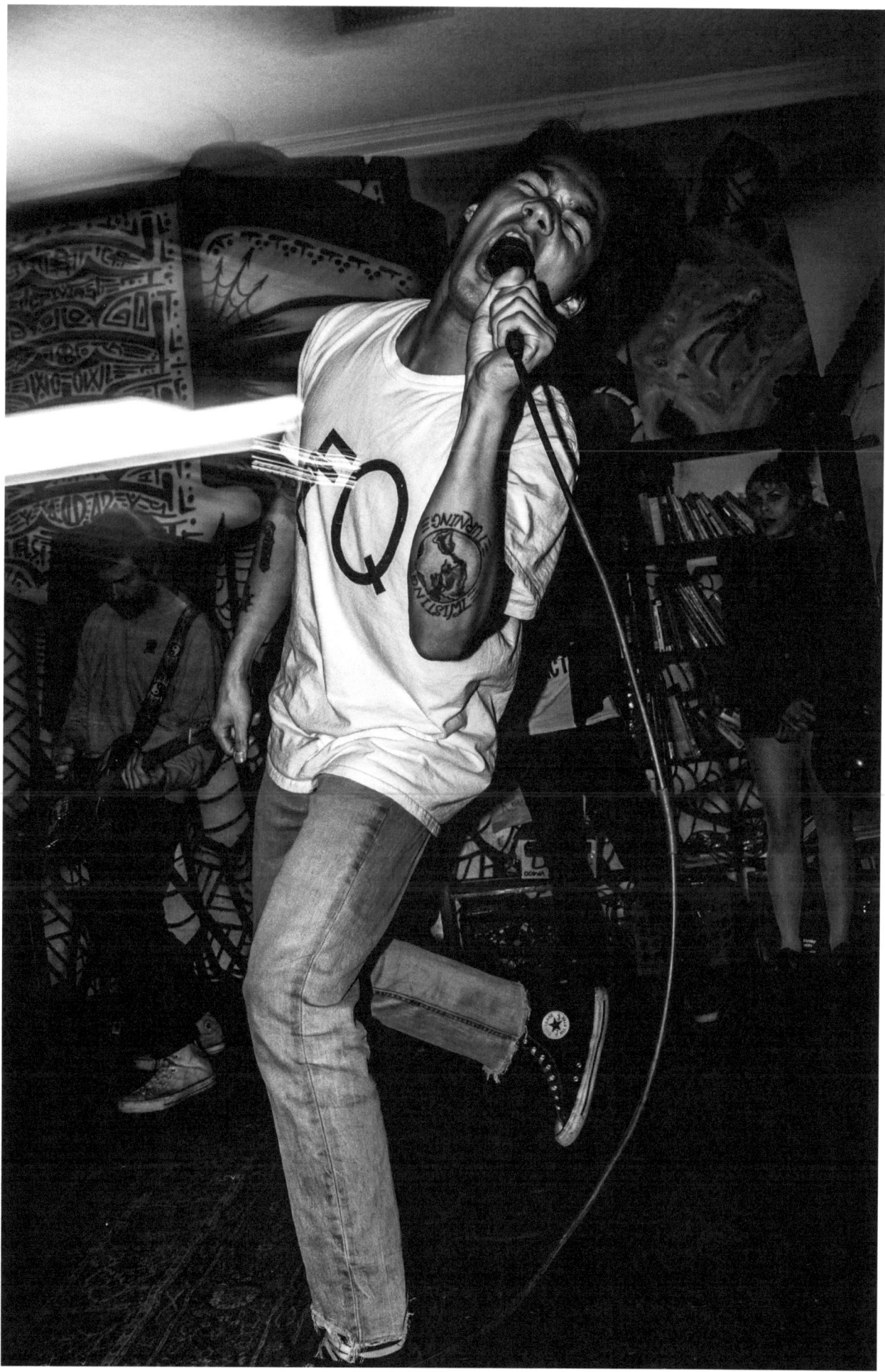

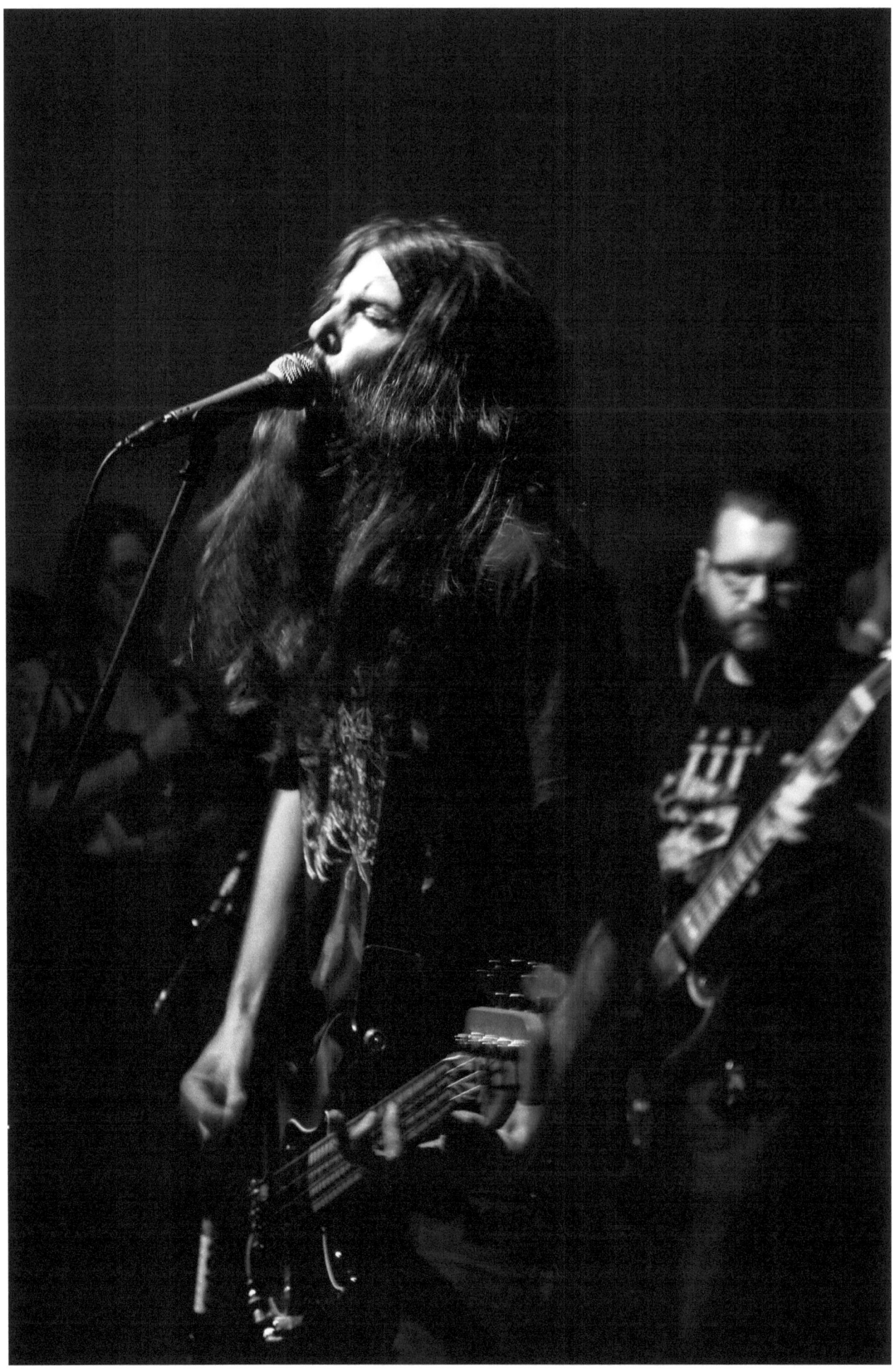

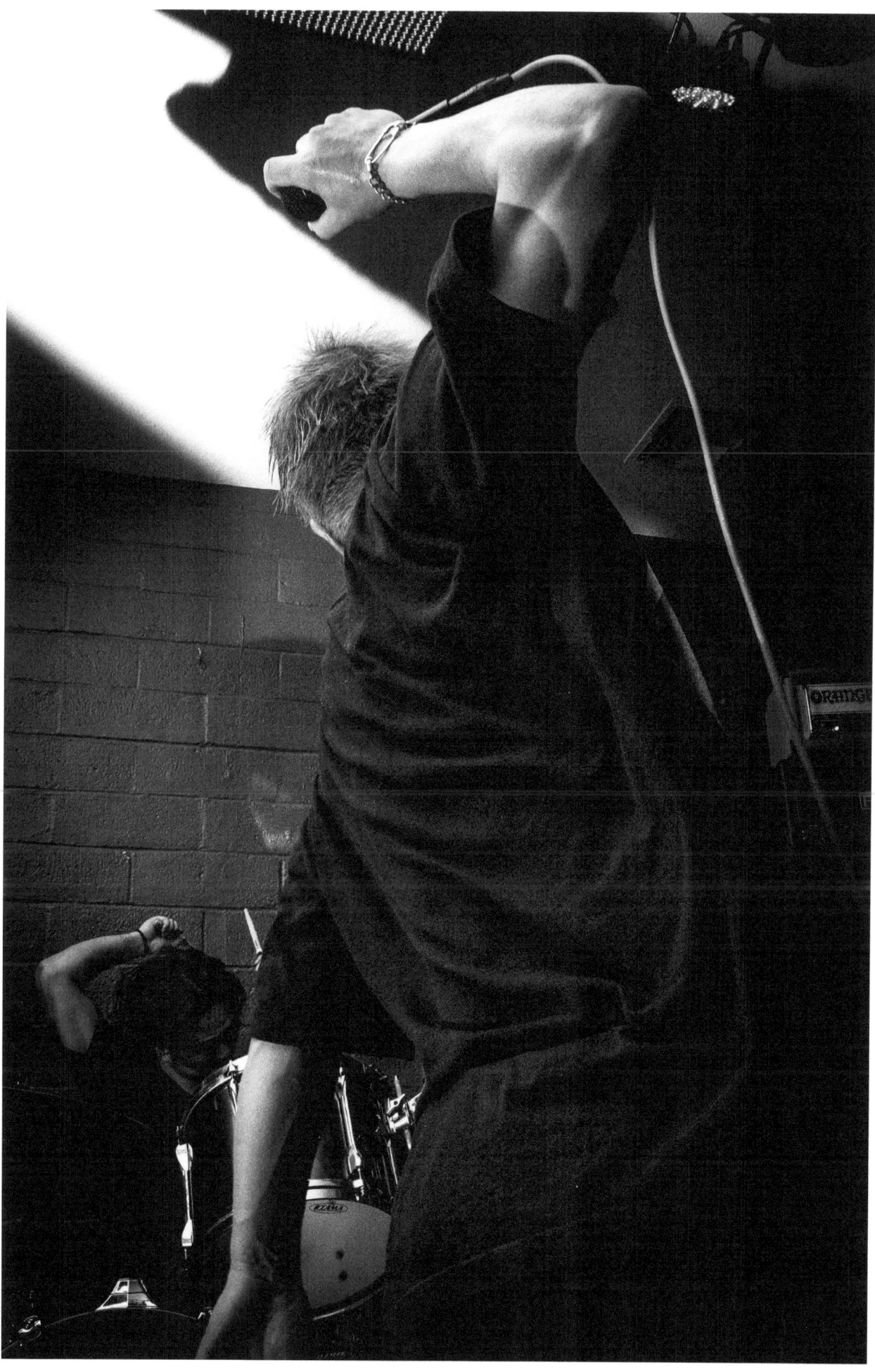

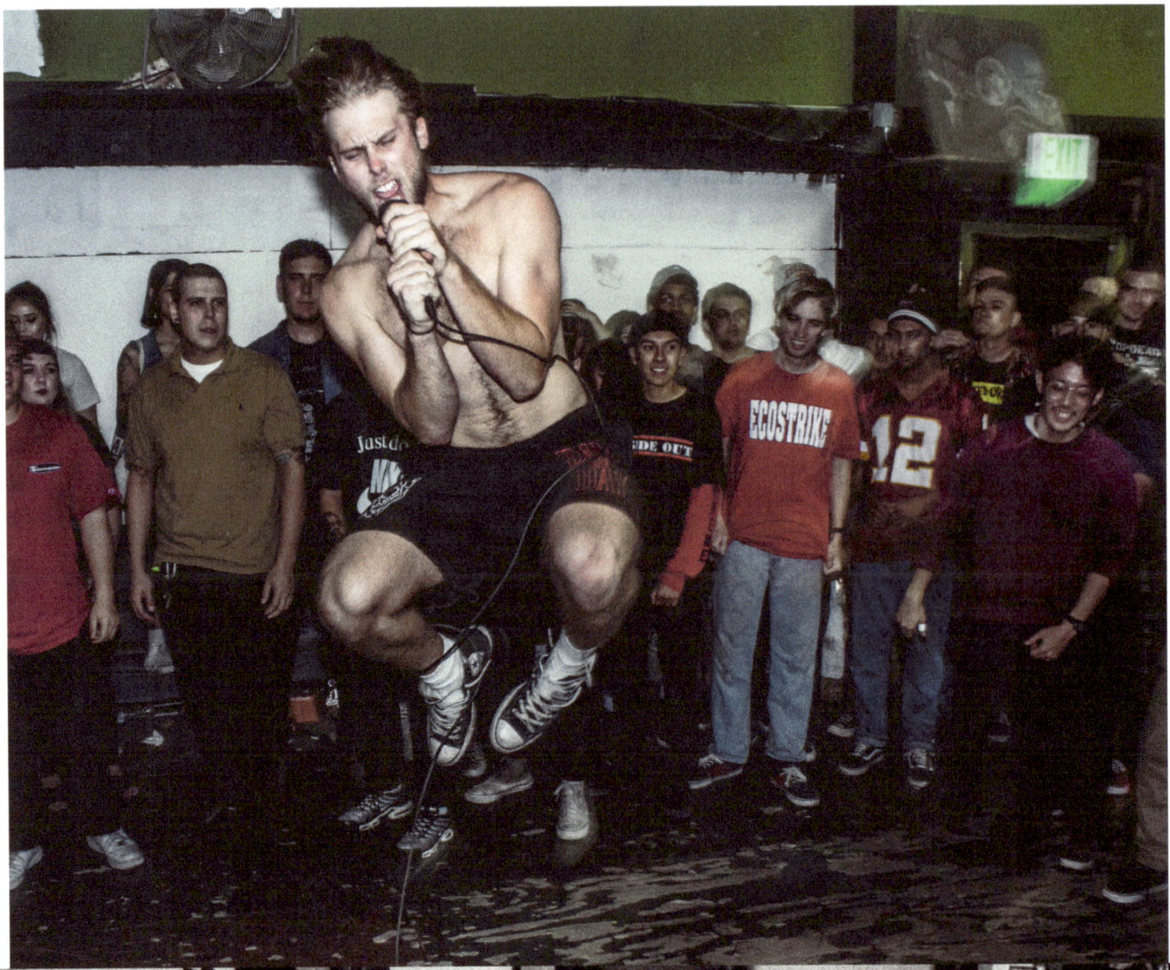

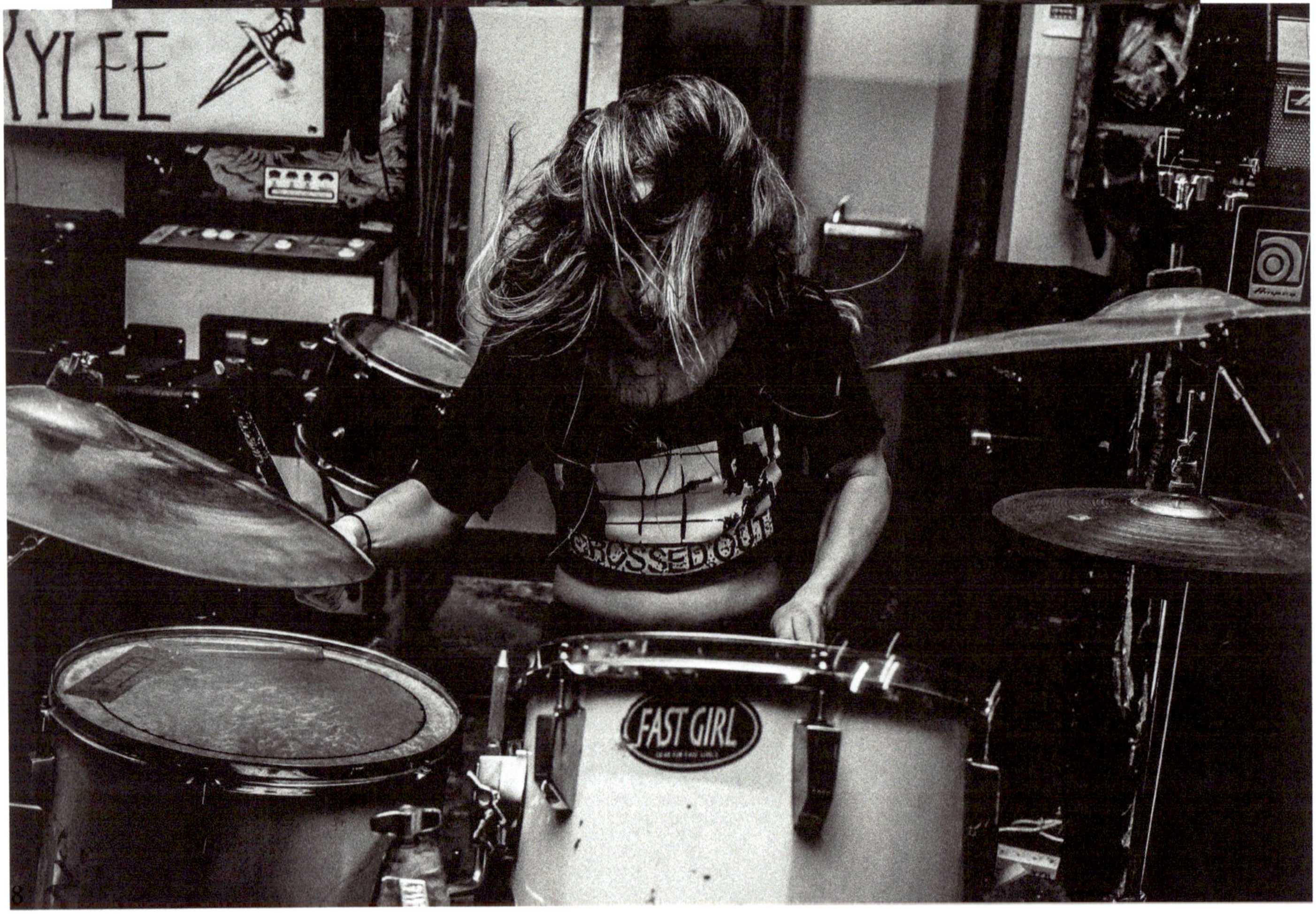

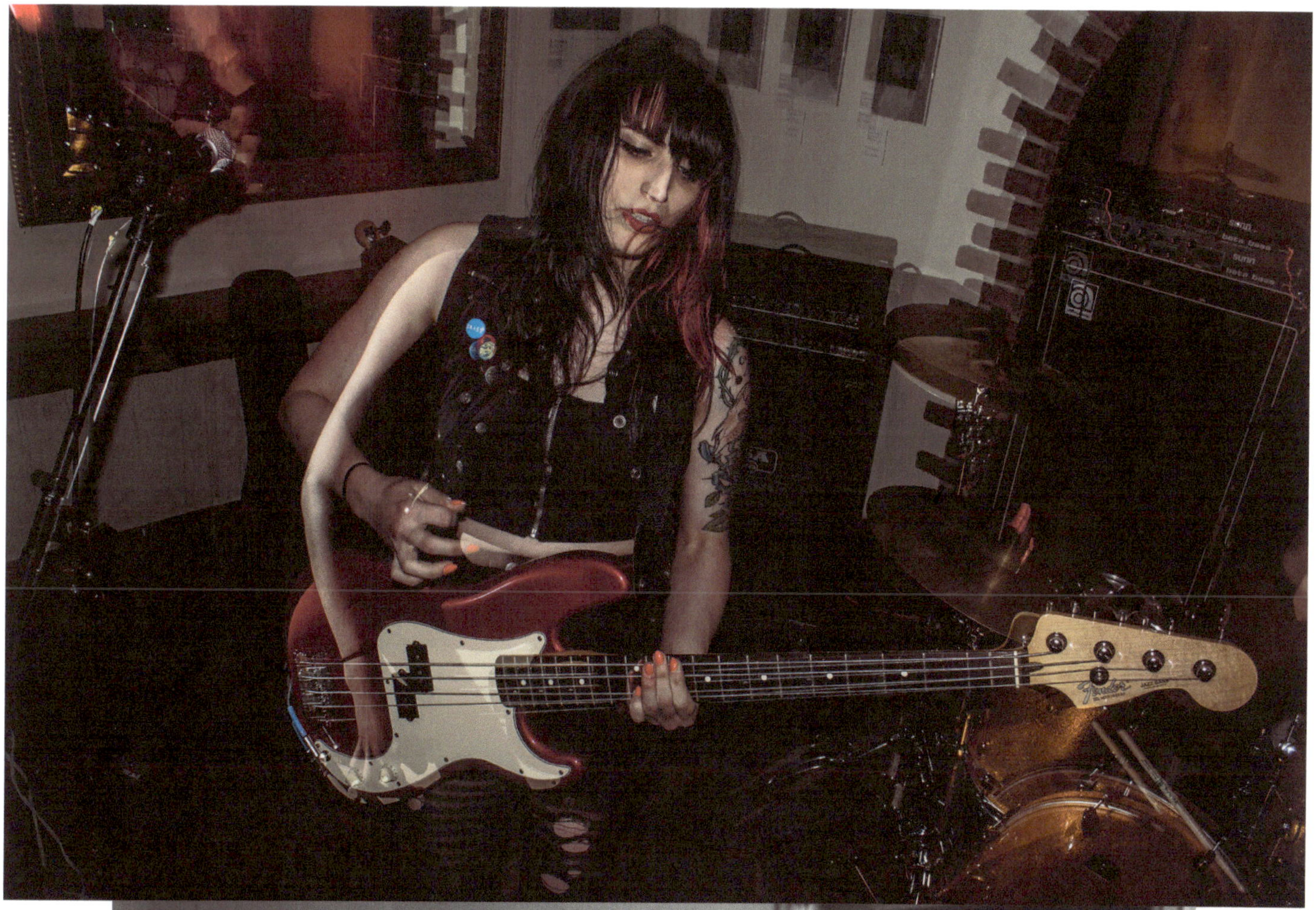

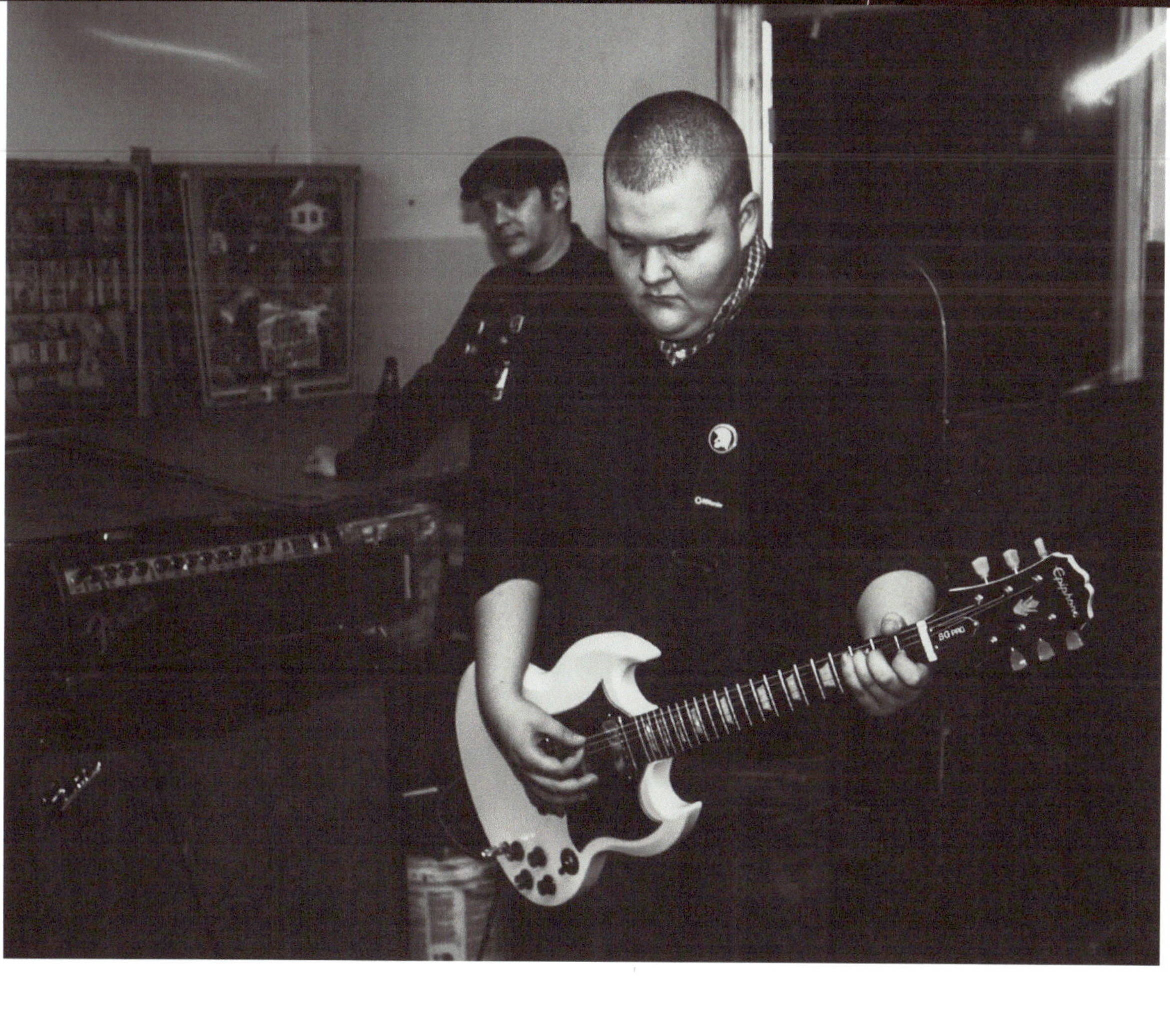

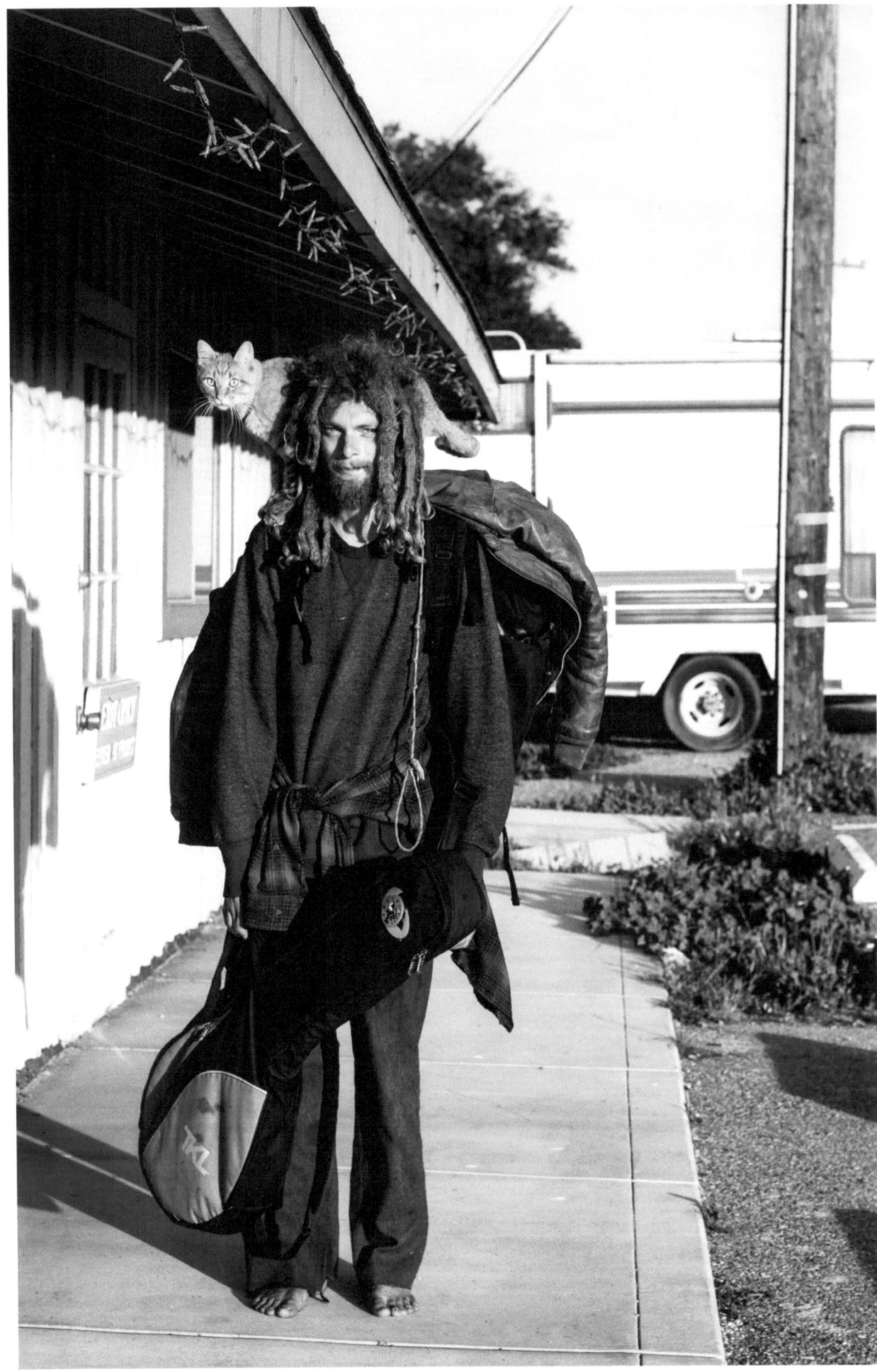

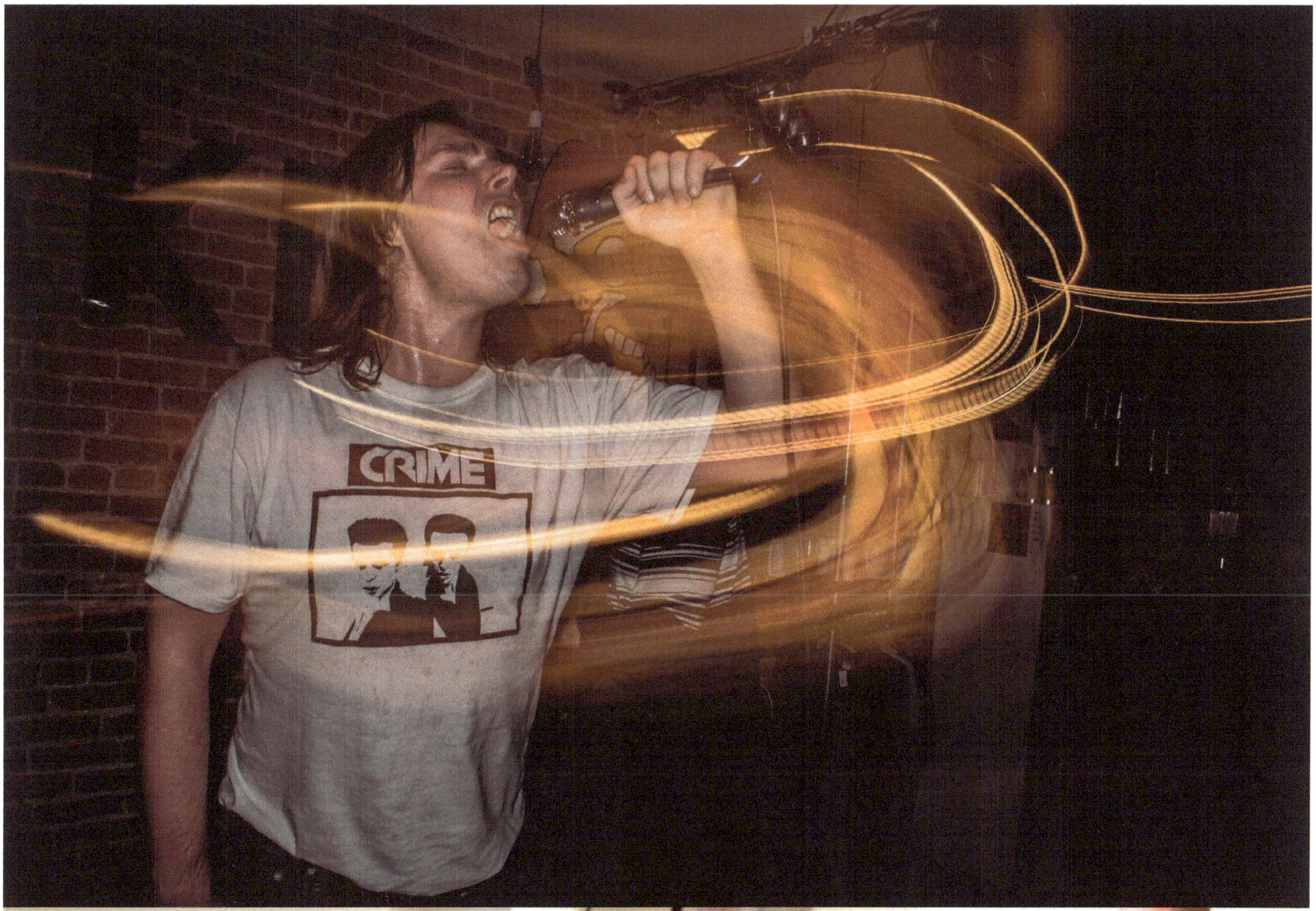

11

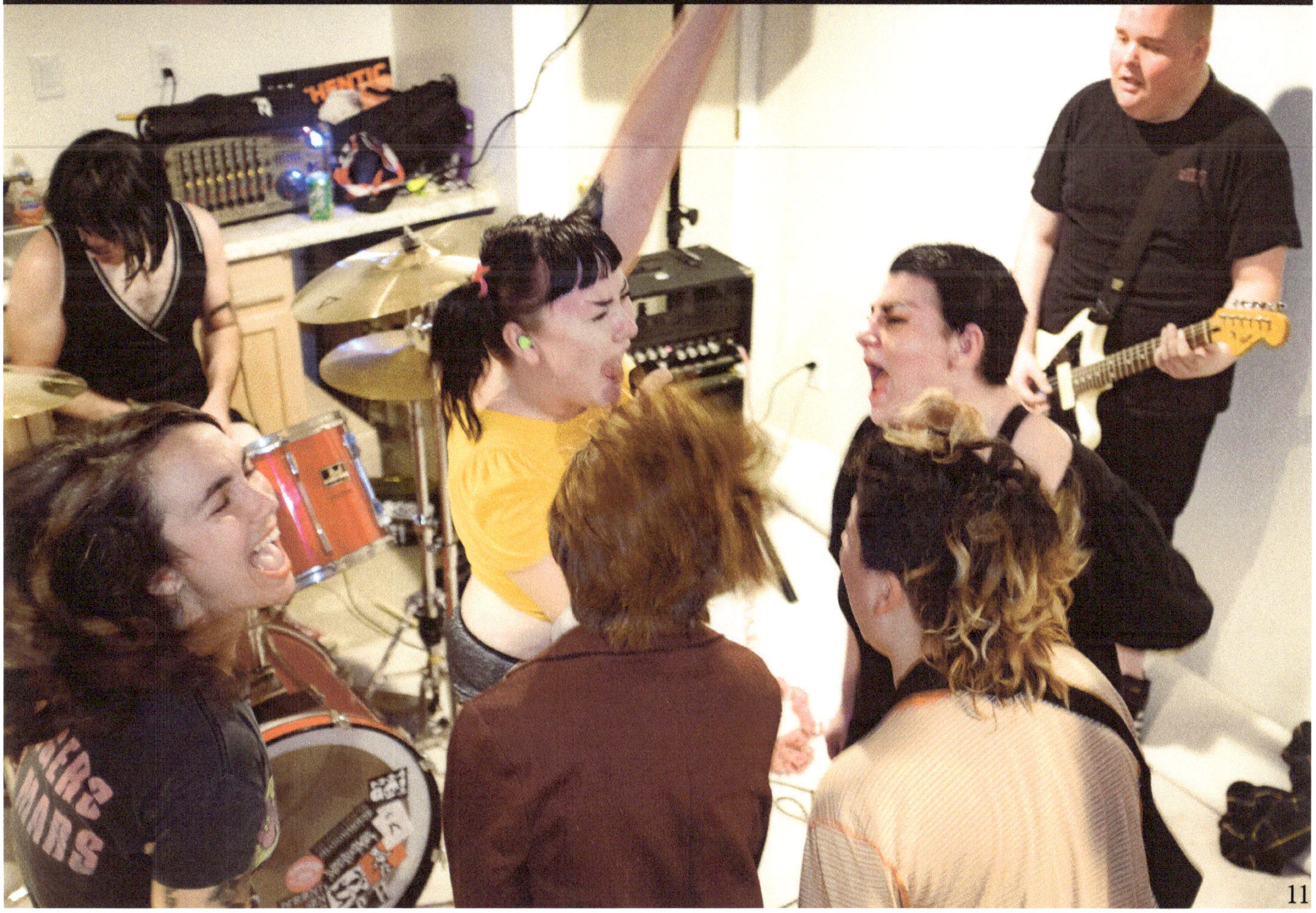

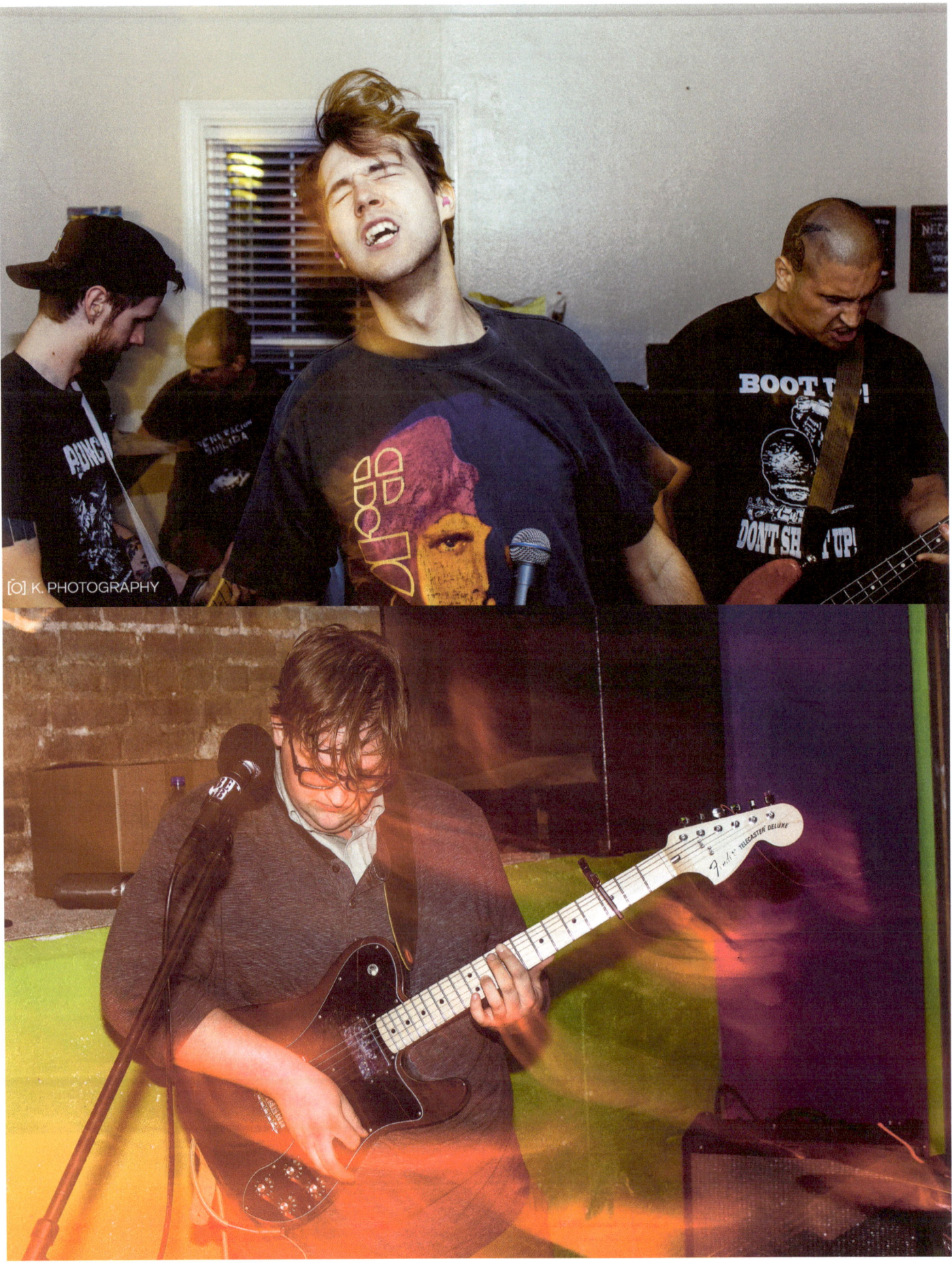

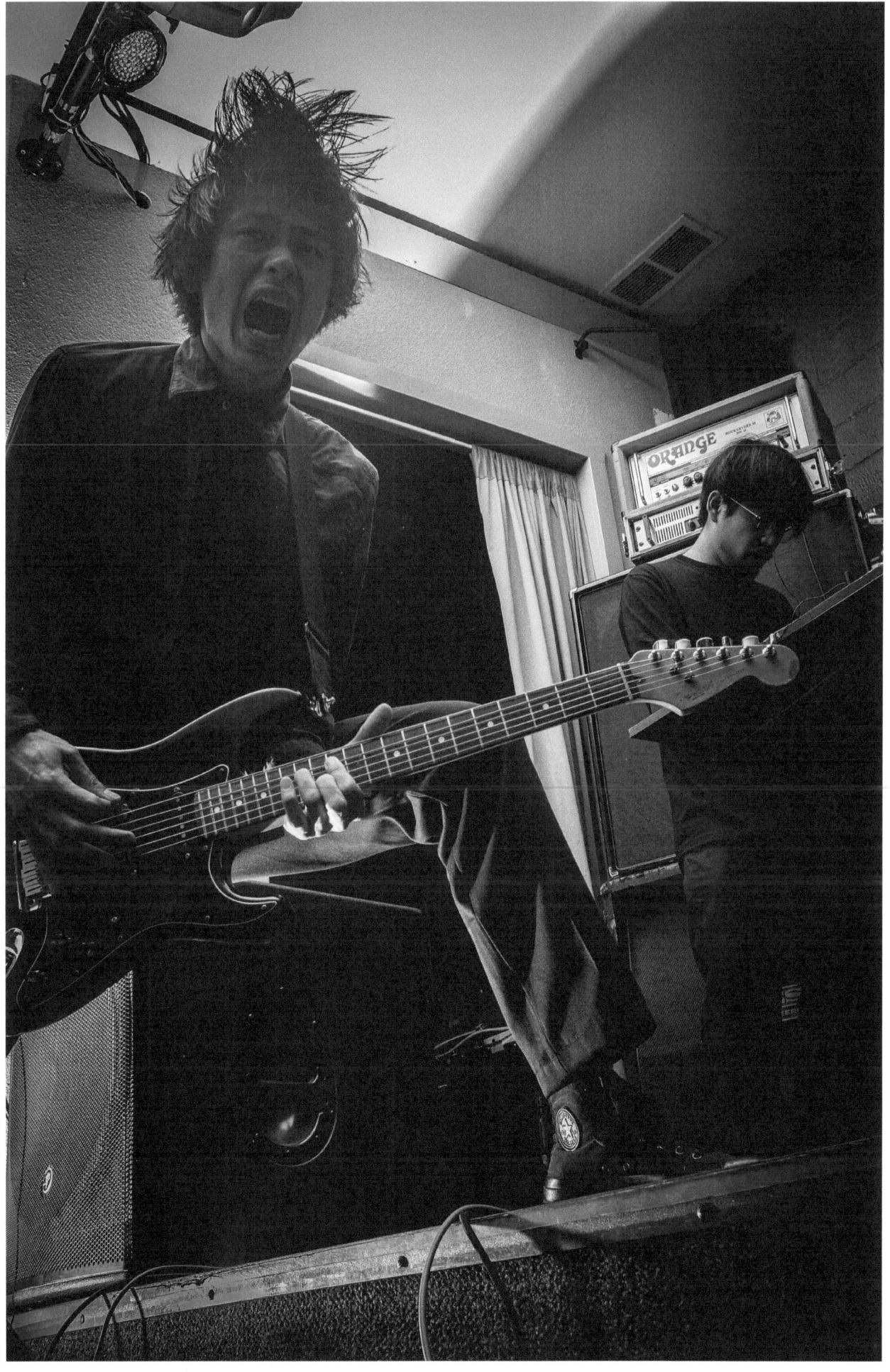

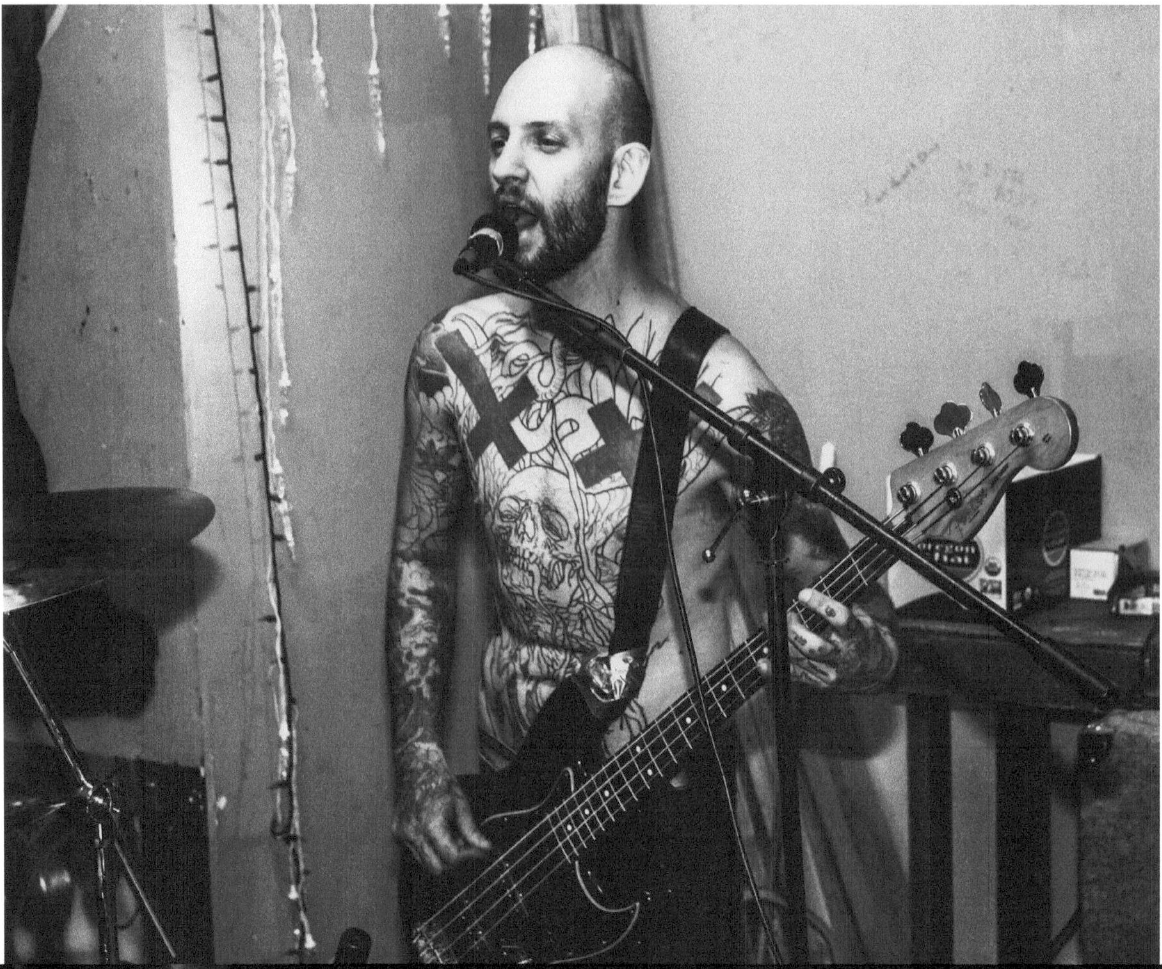

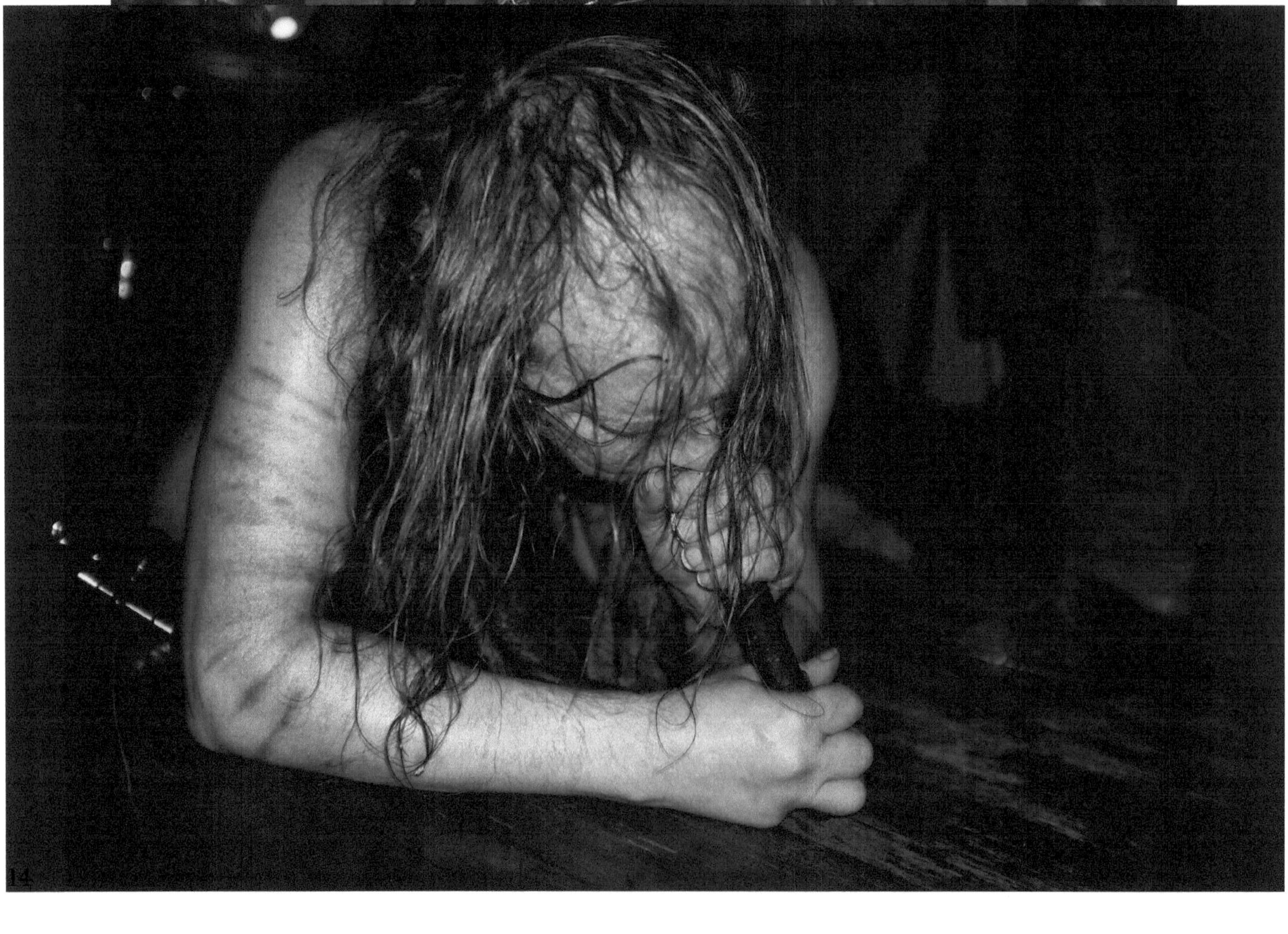

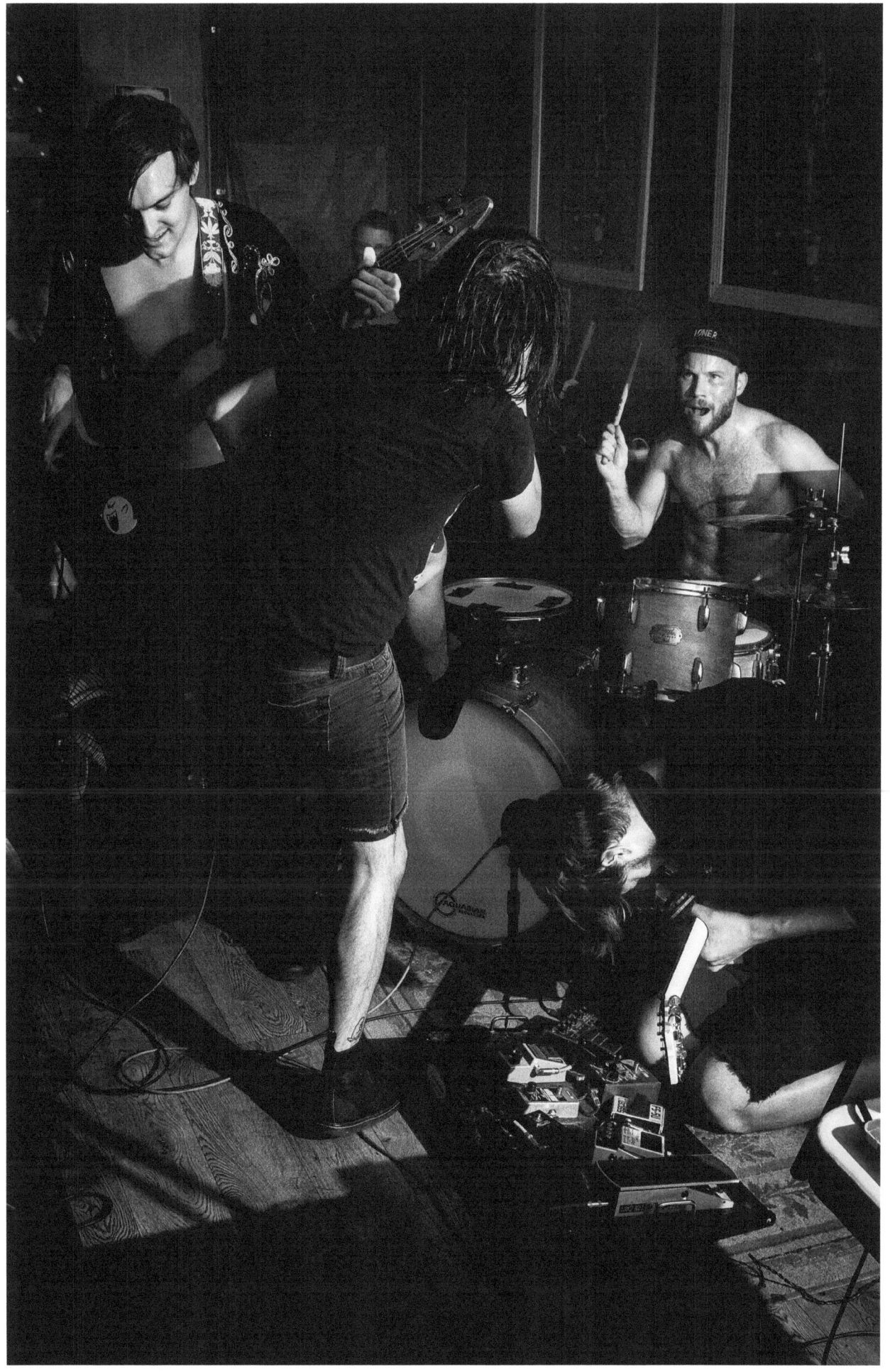

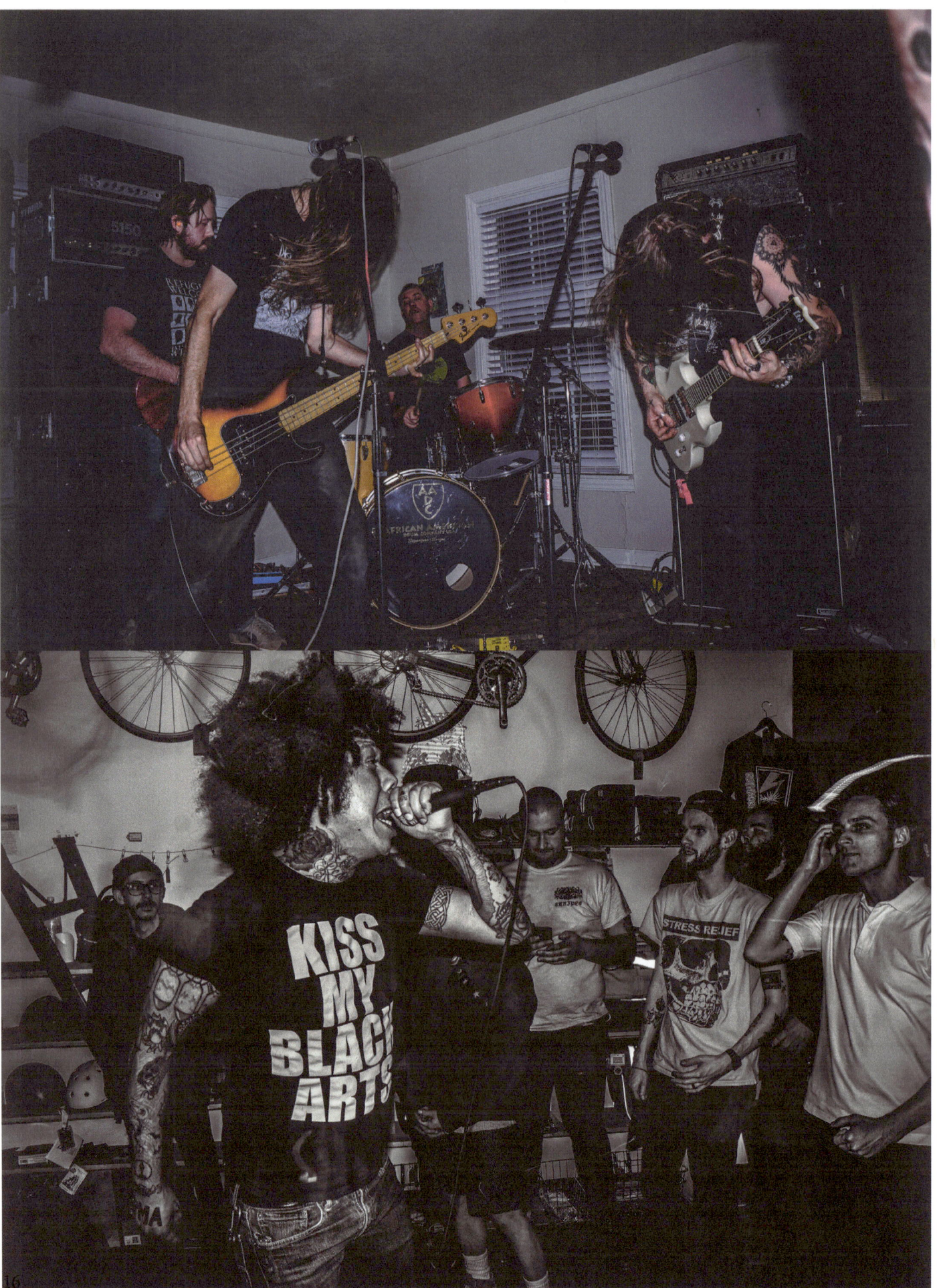

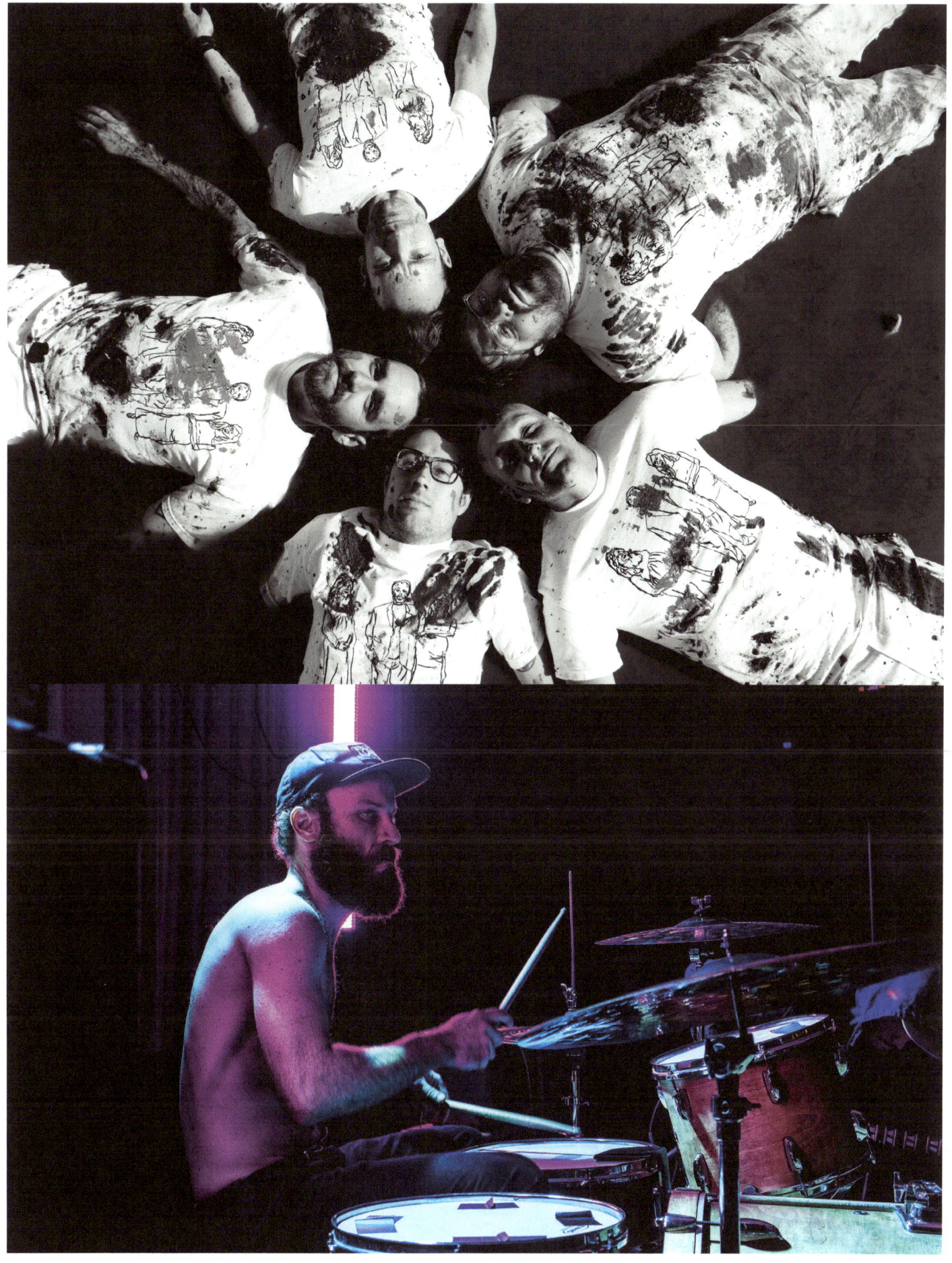

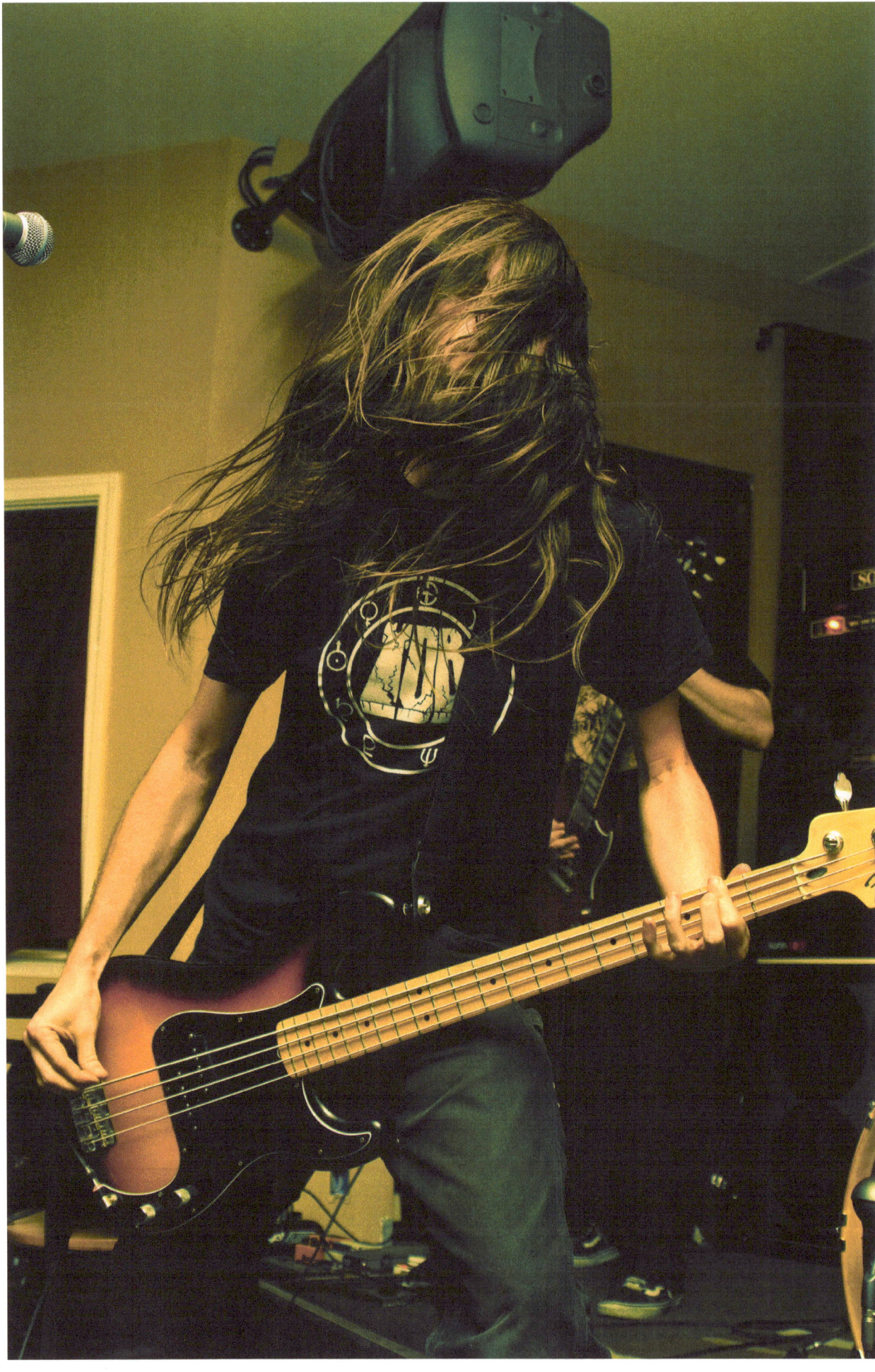

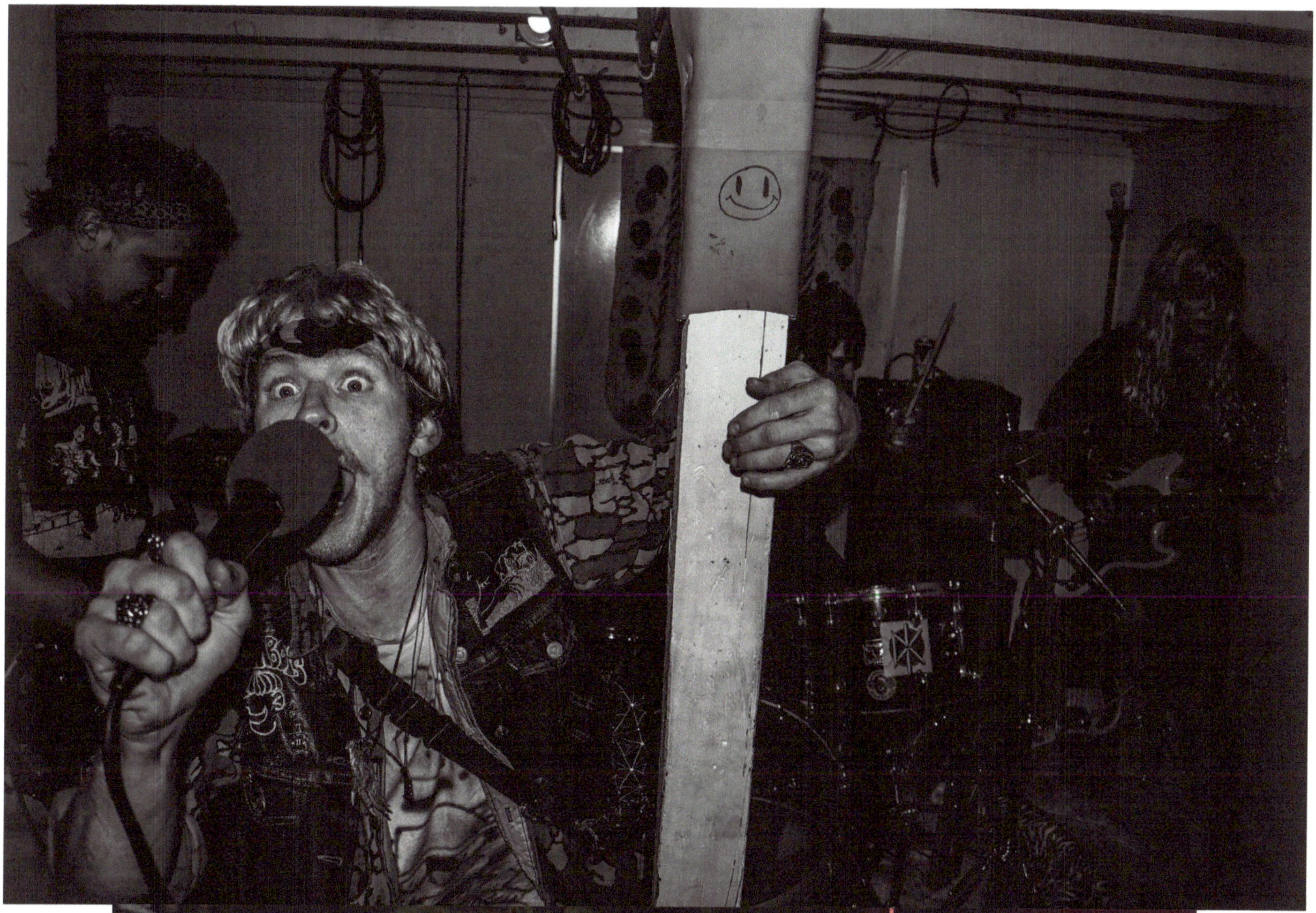

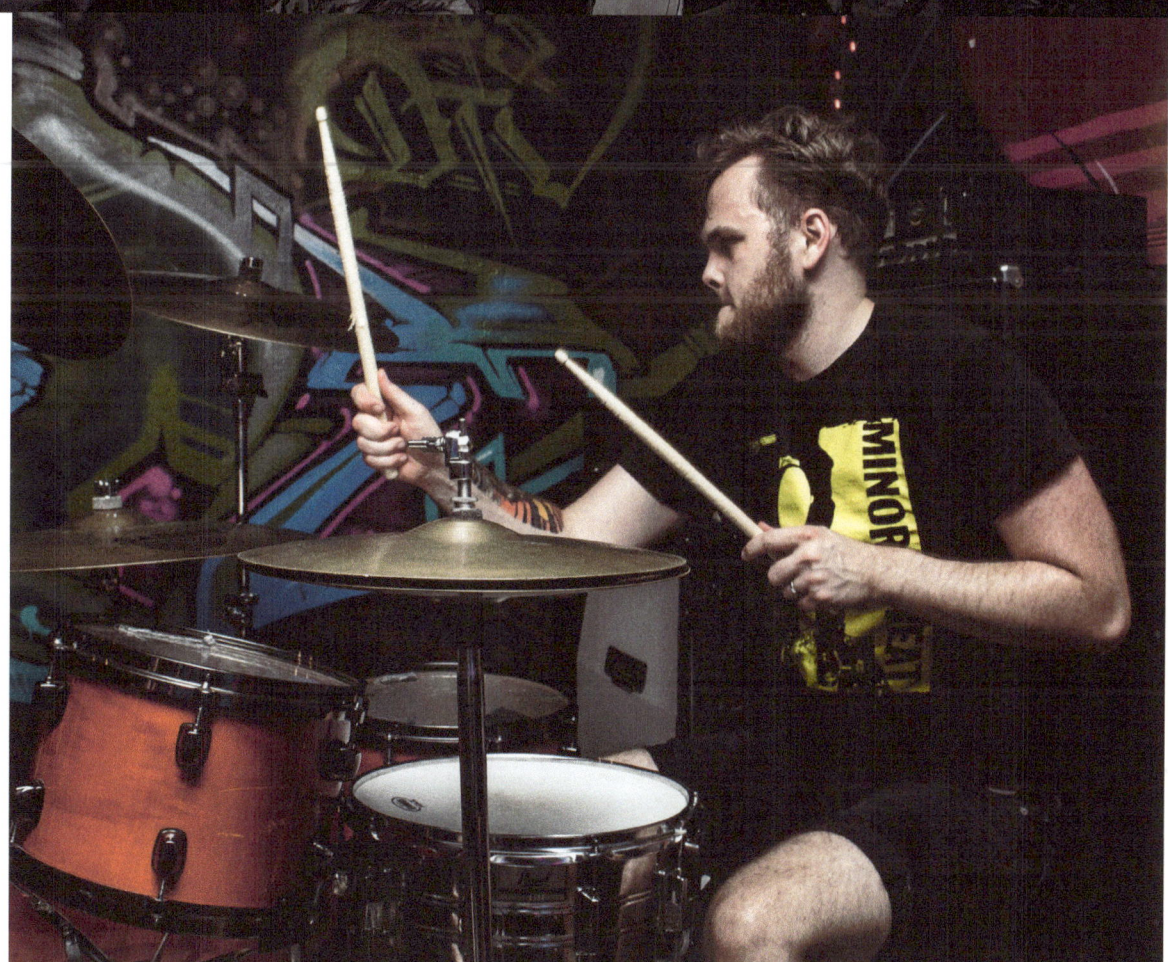

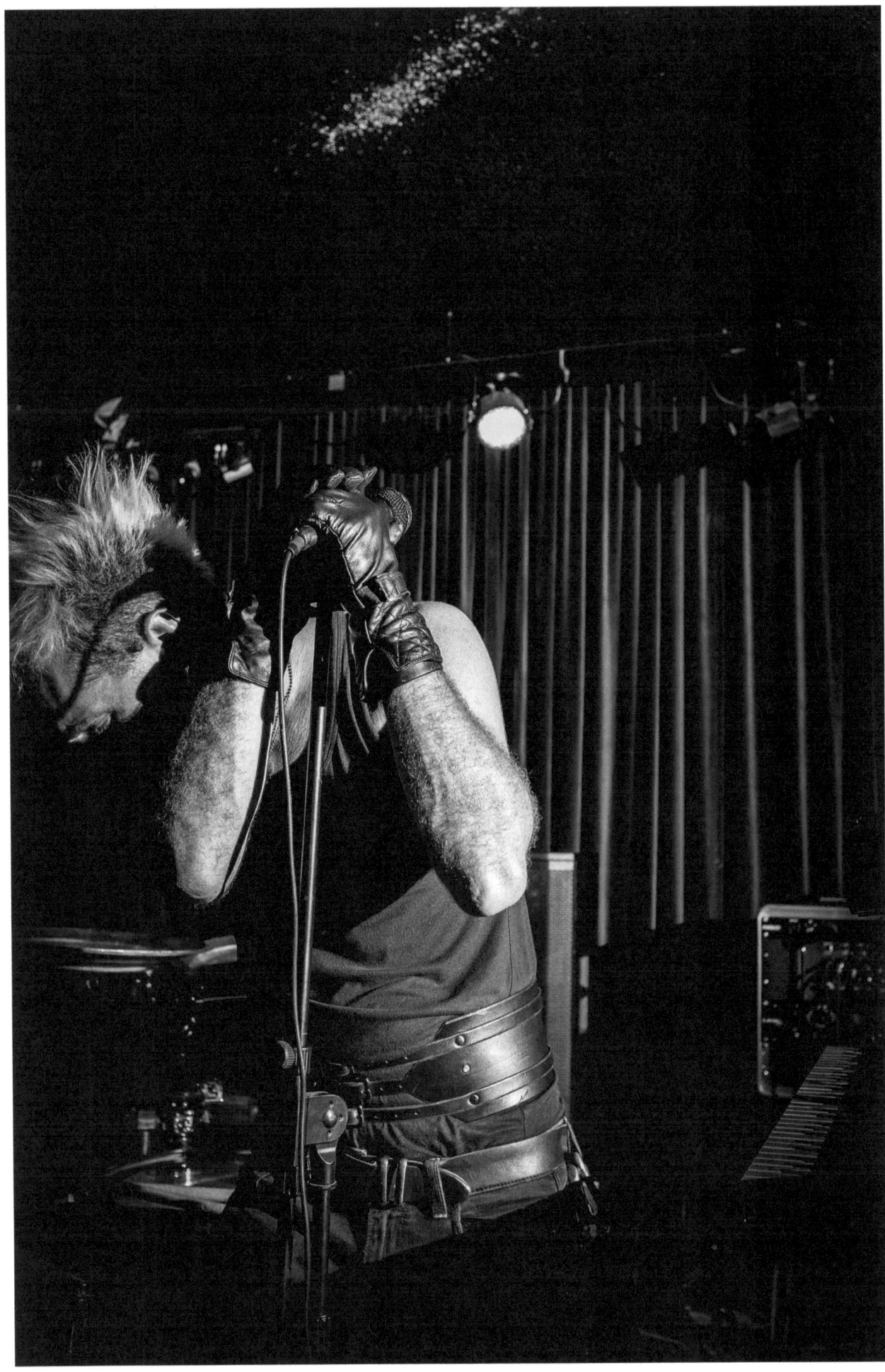

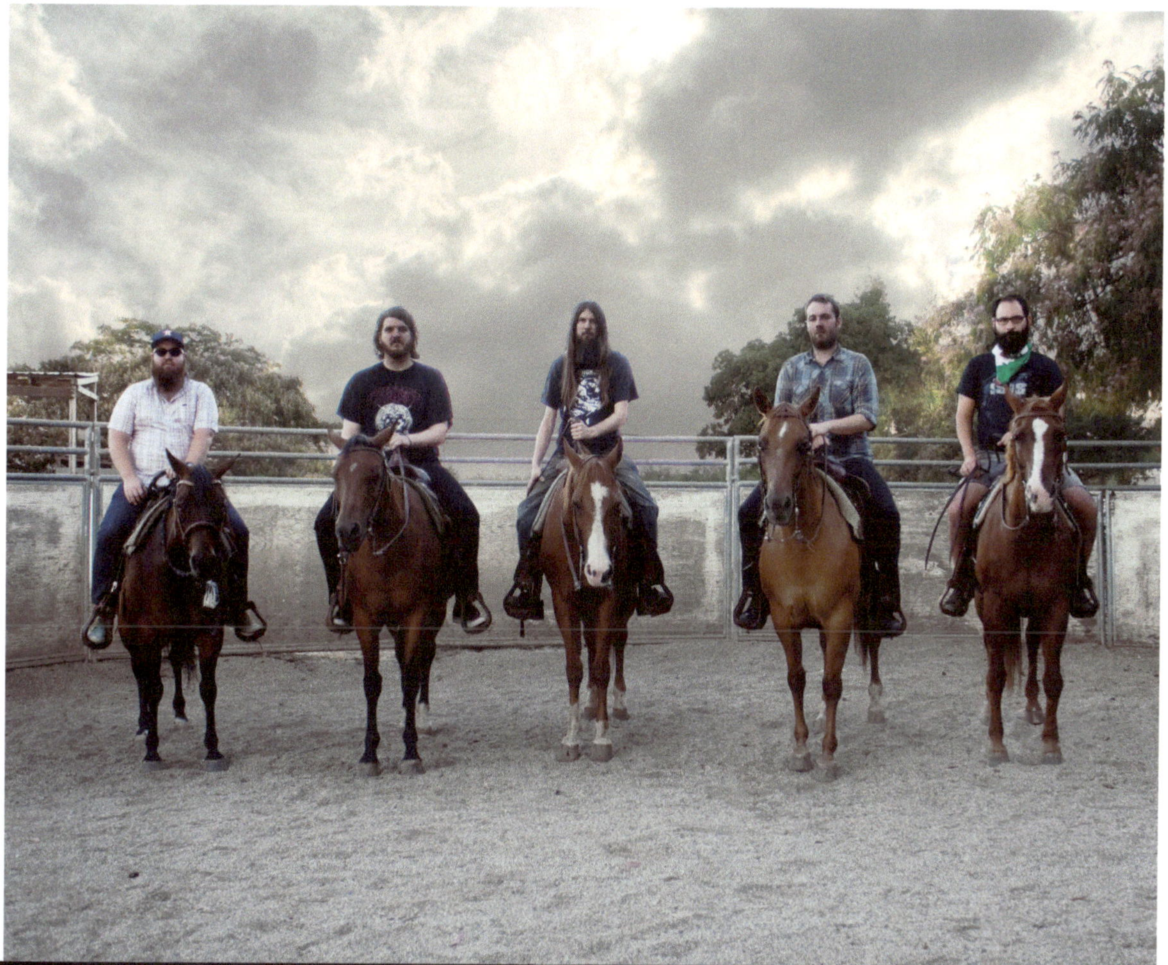

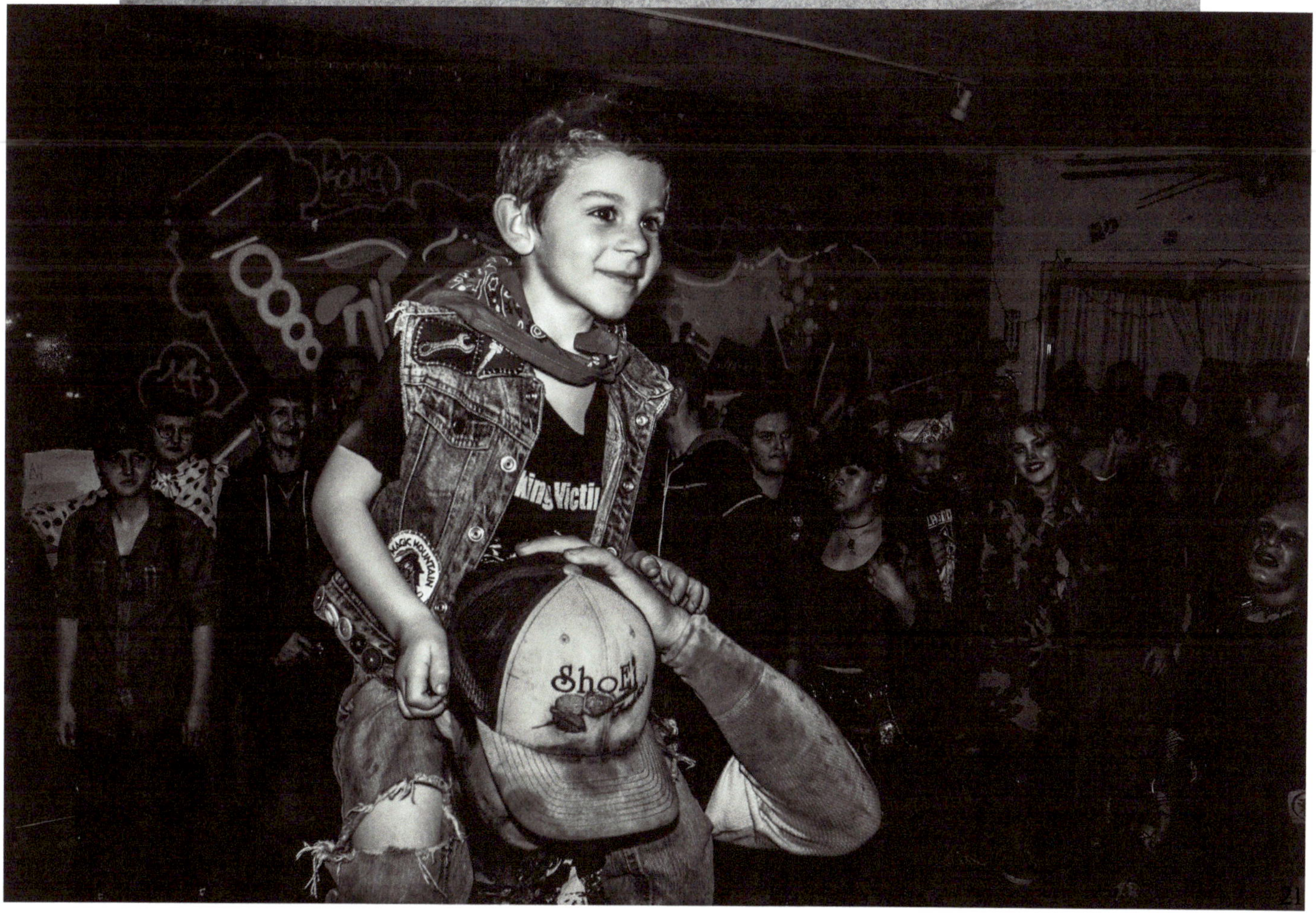

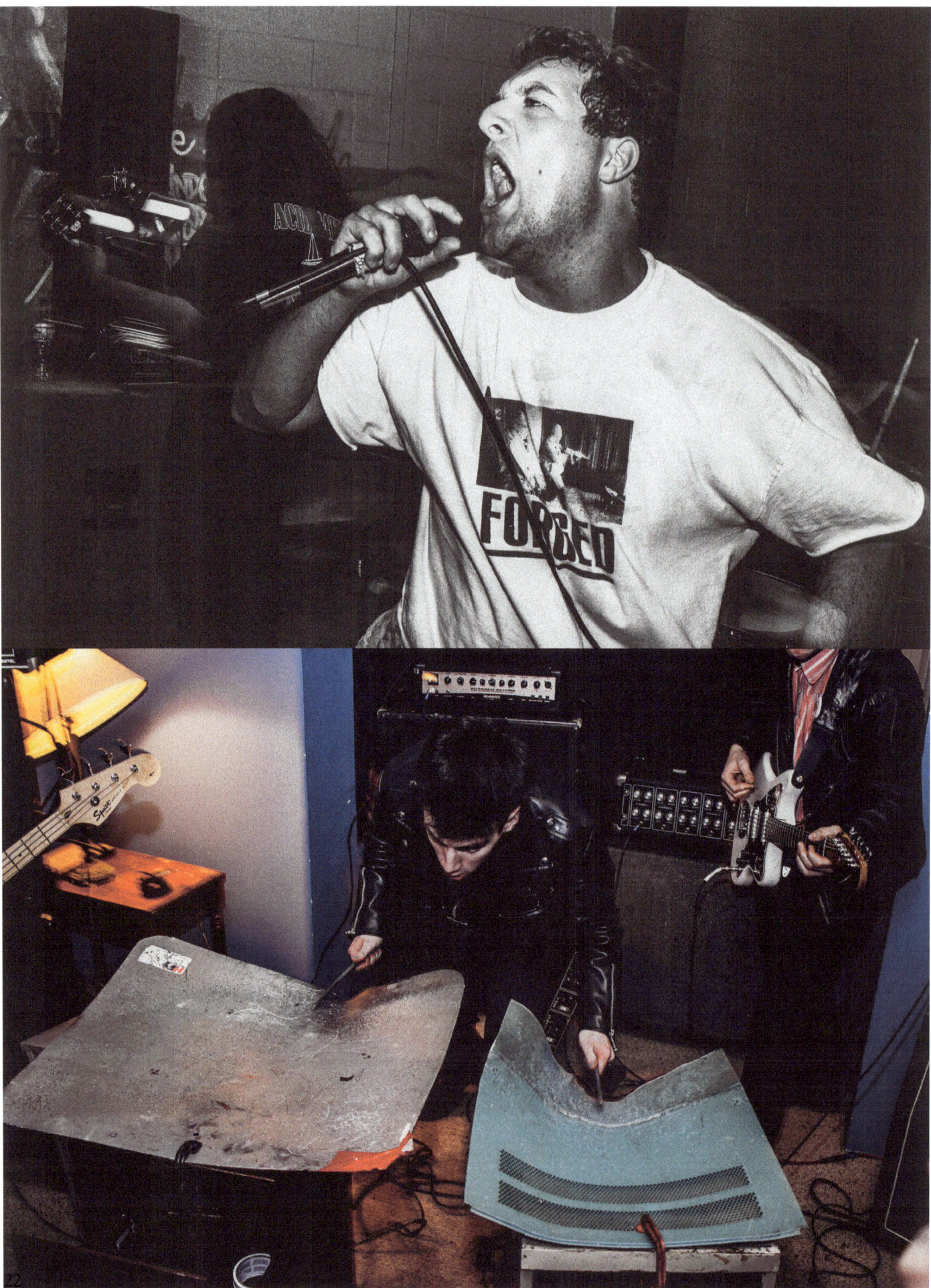

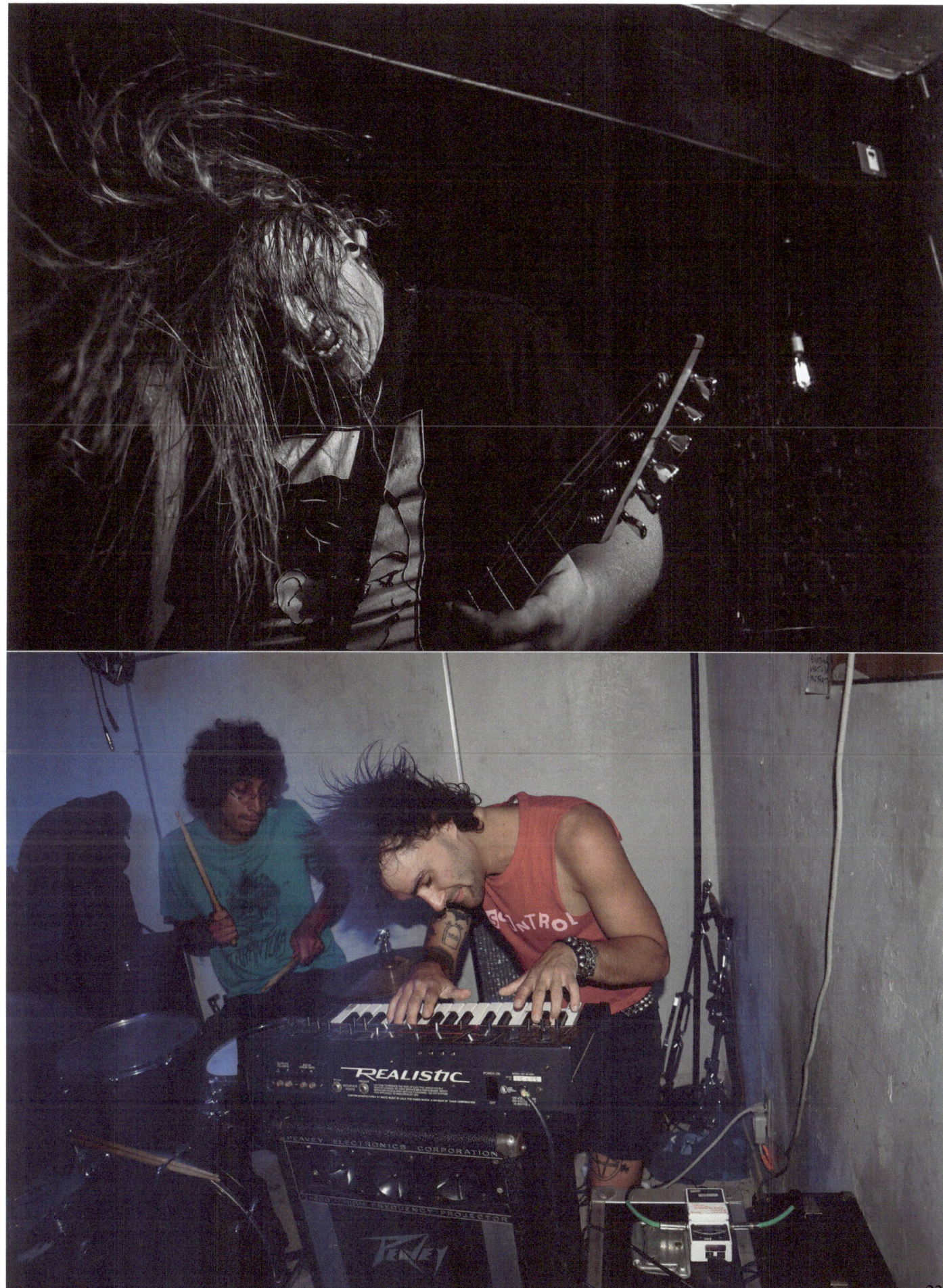

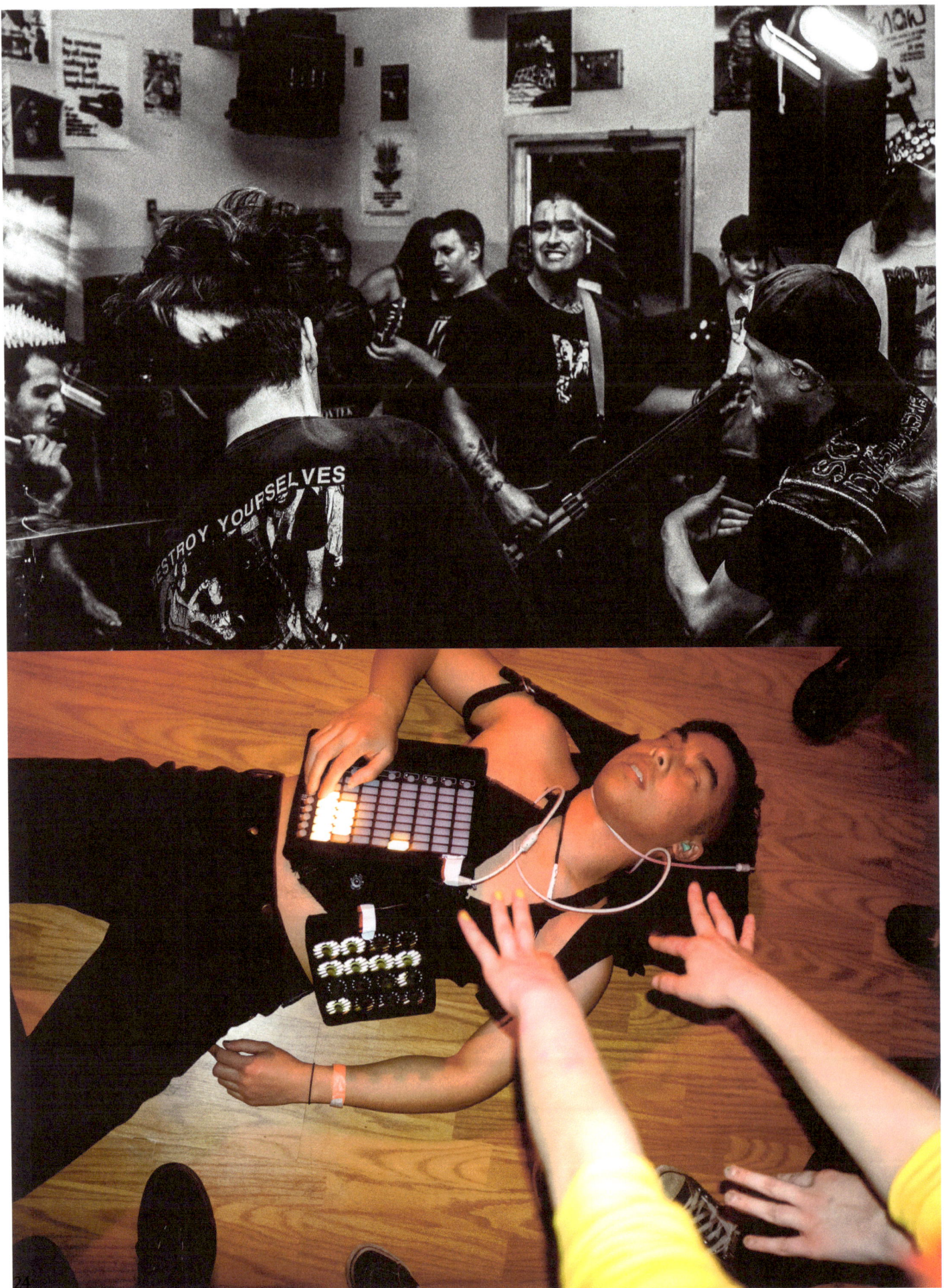

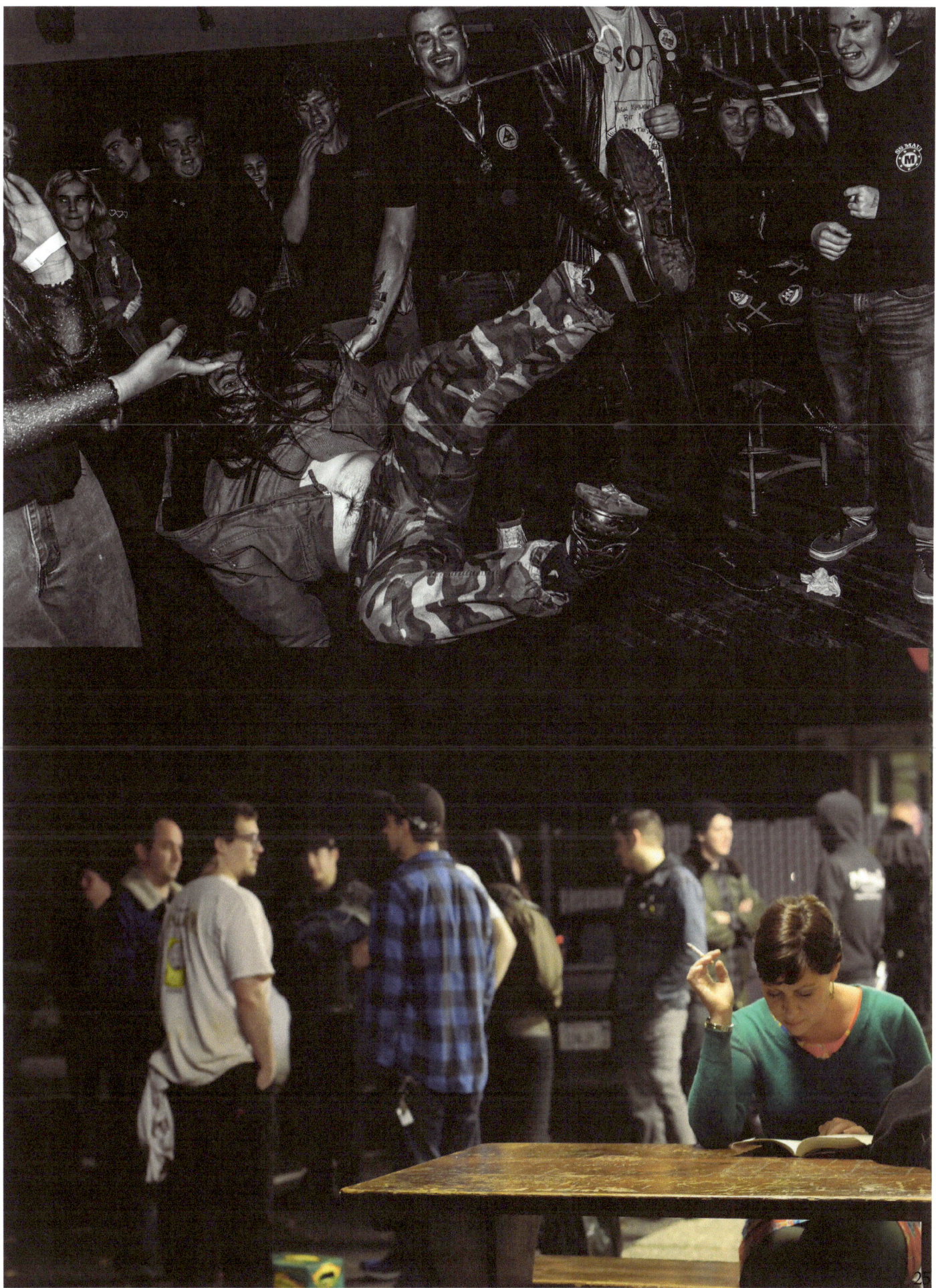

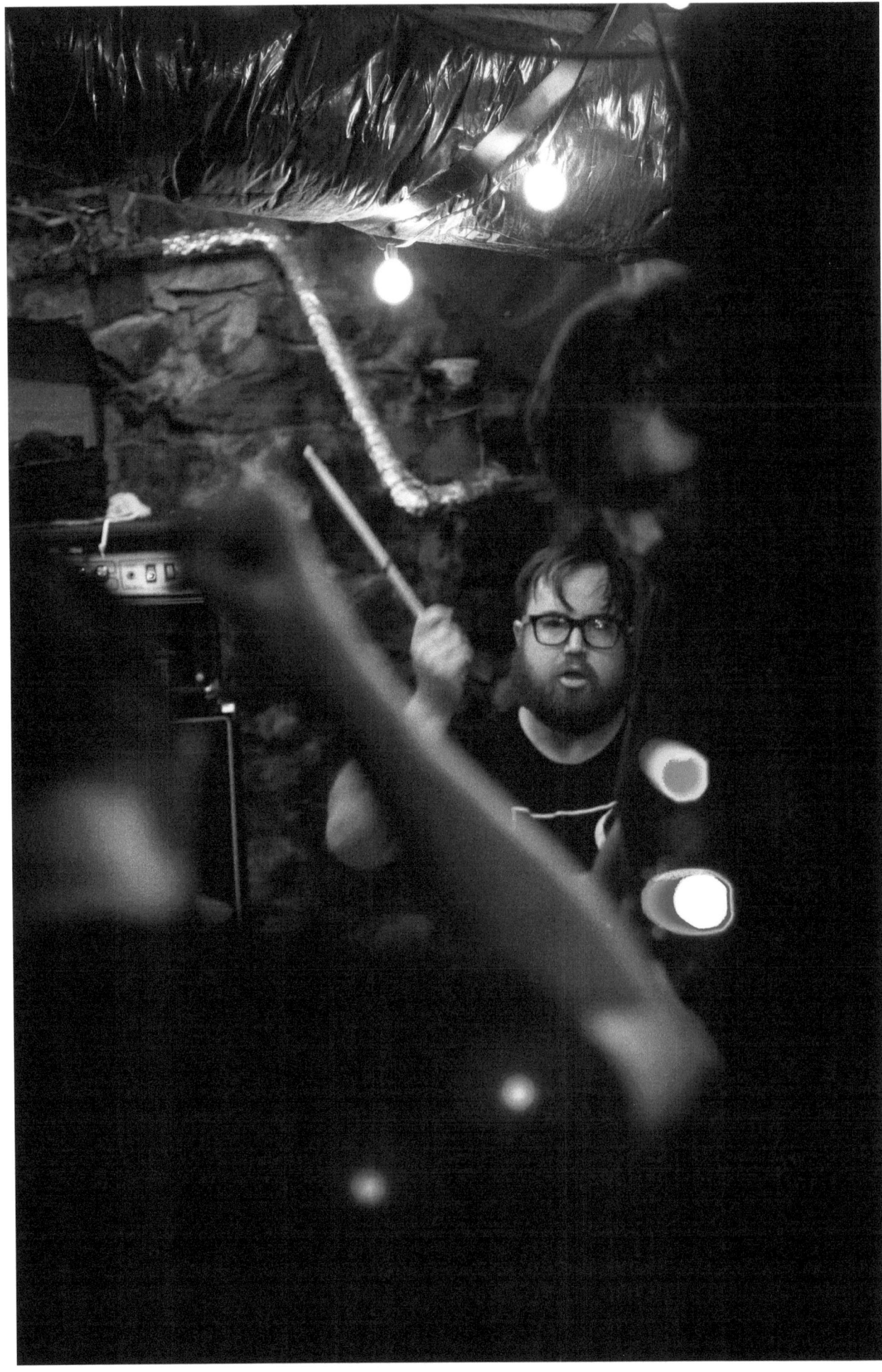

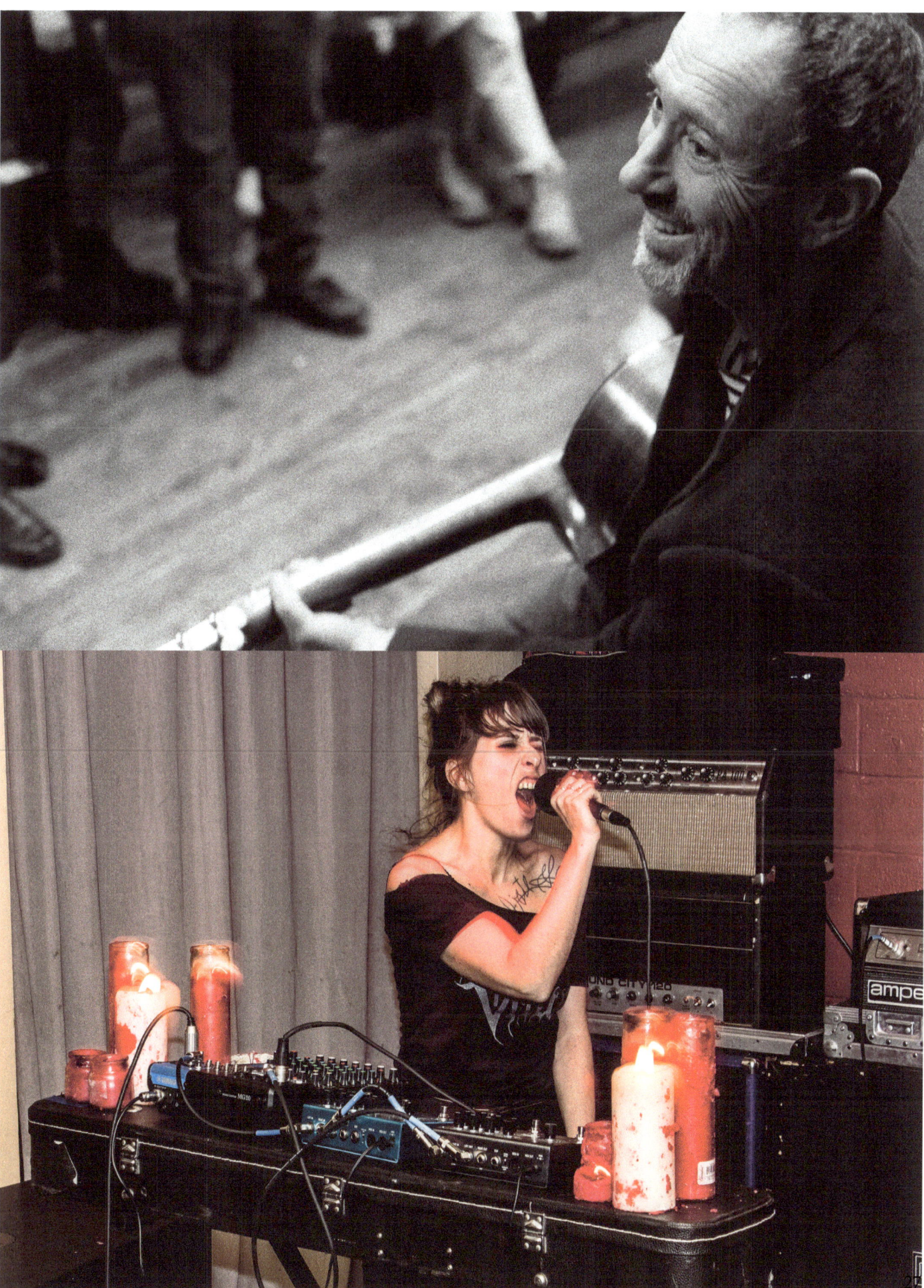

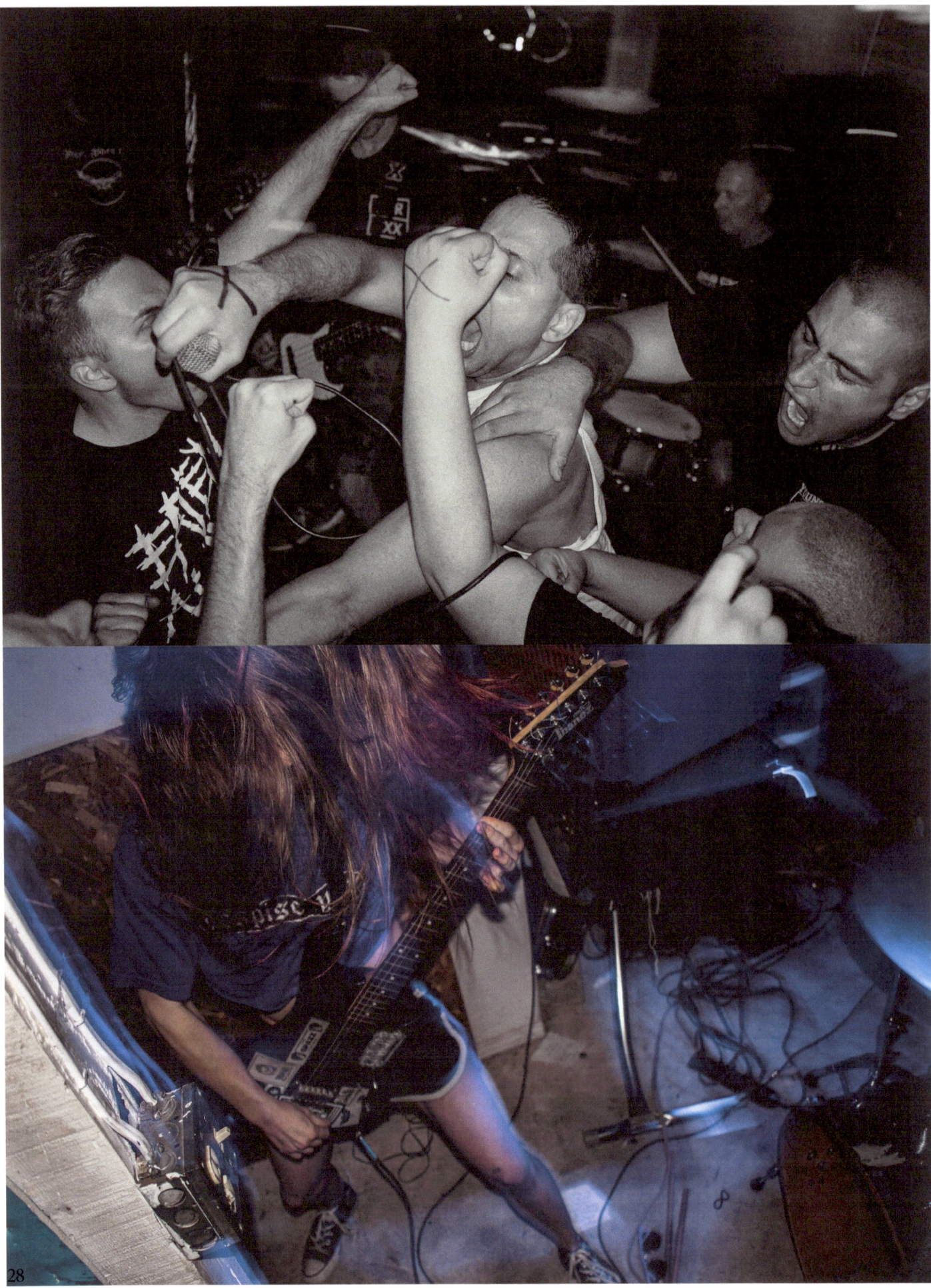

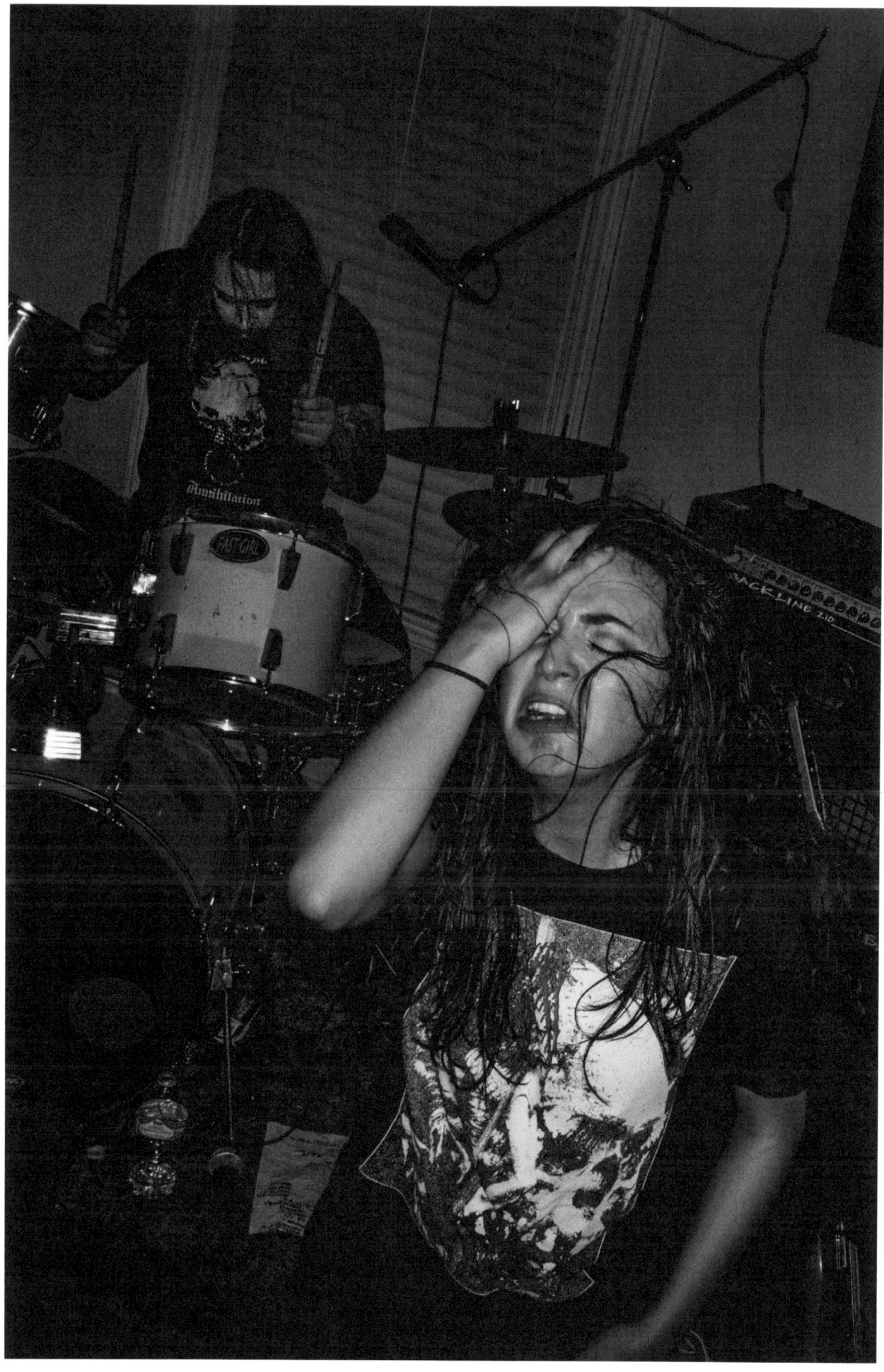

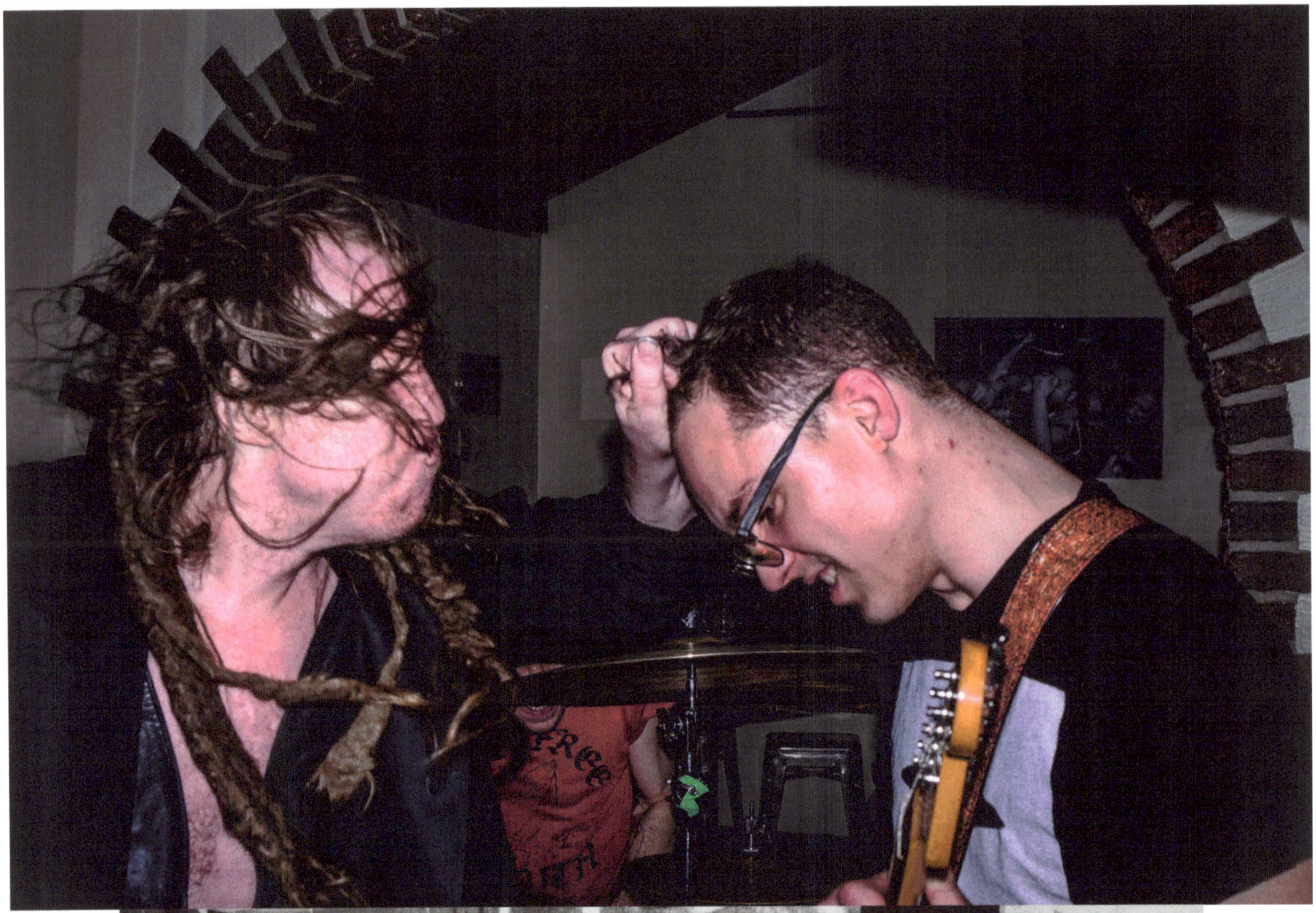

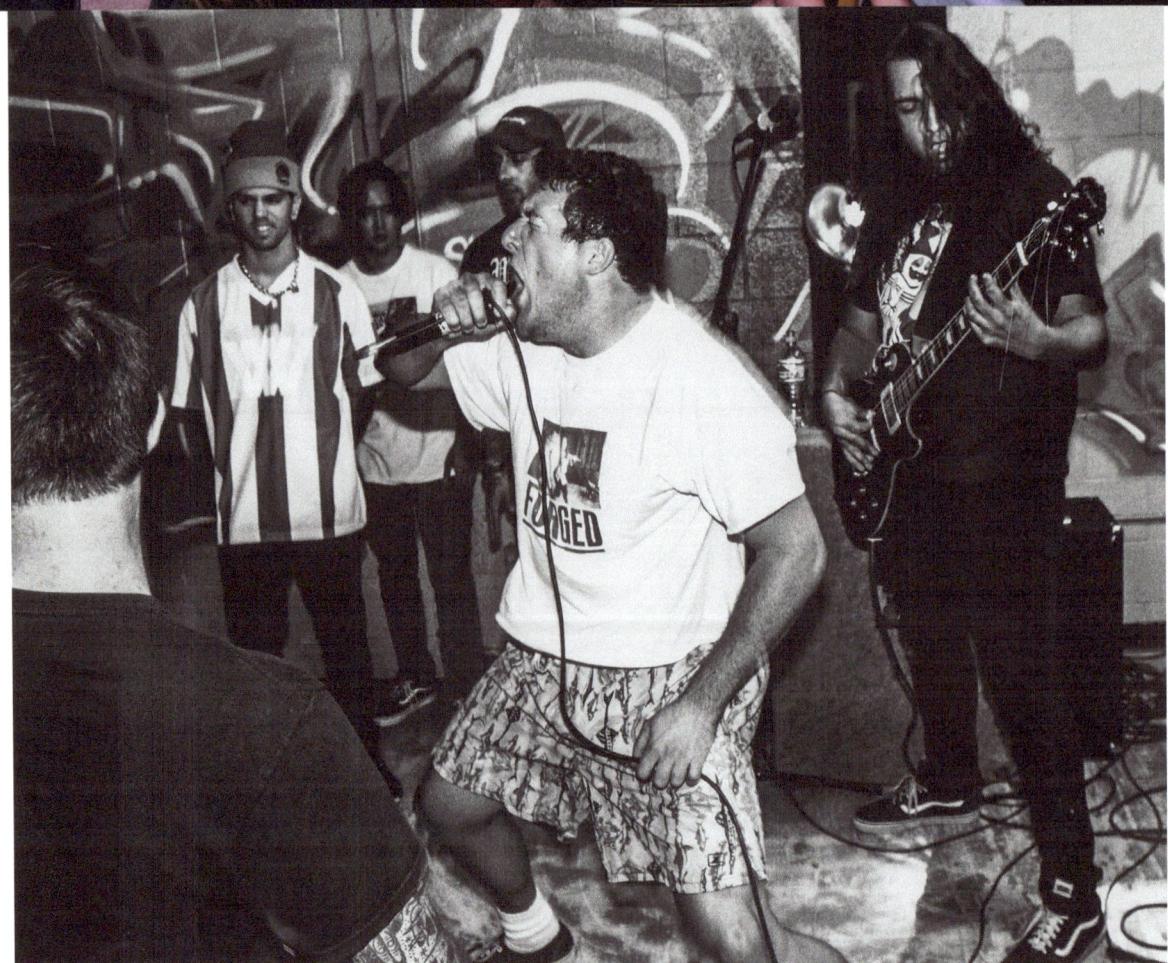

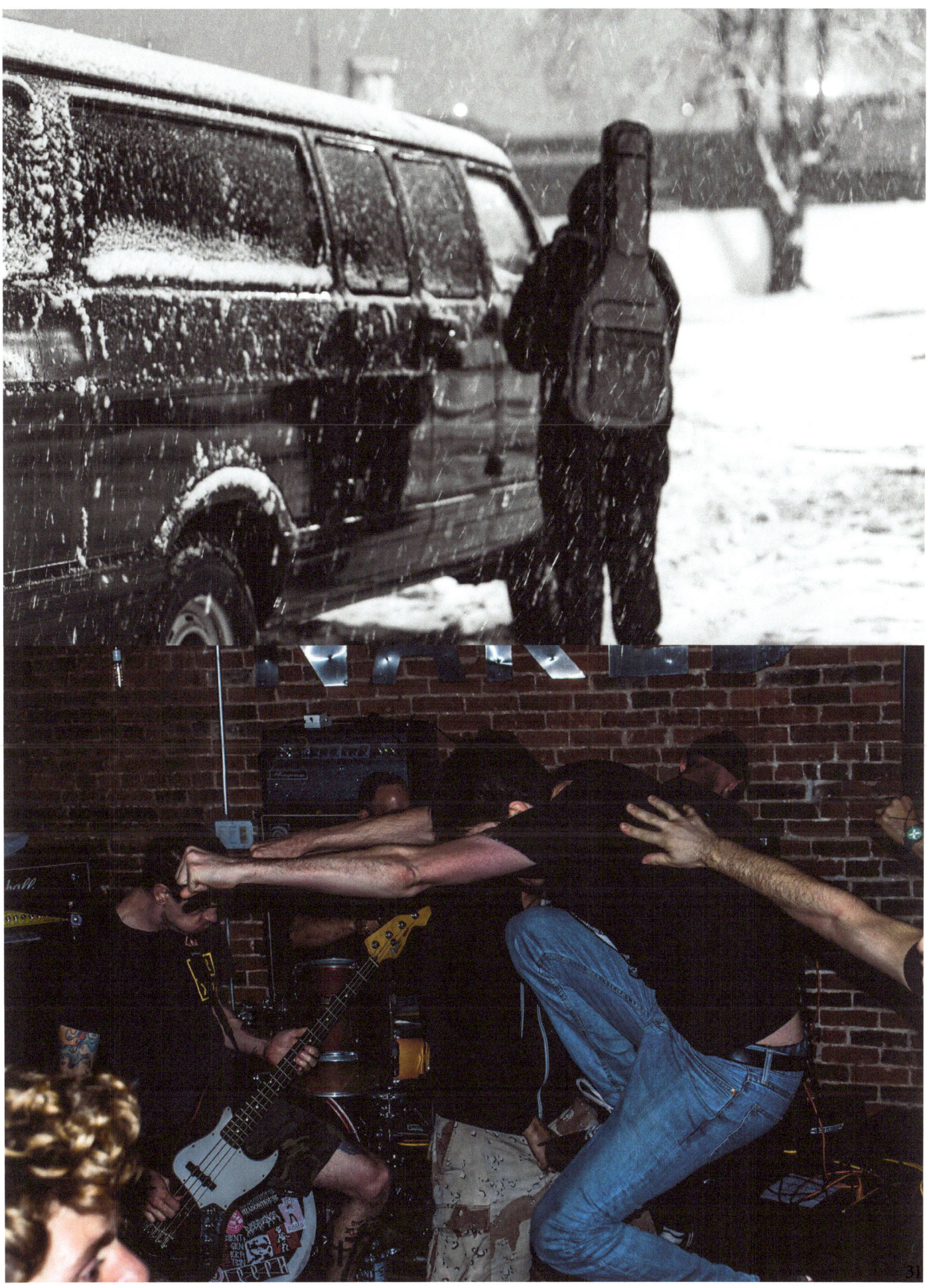

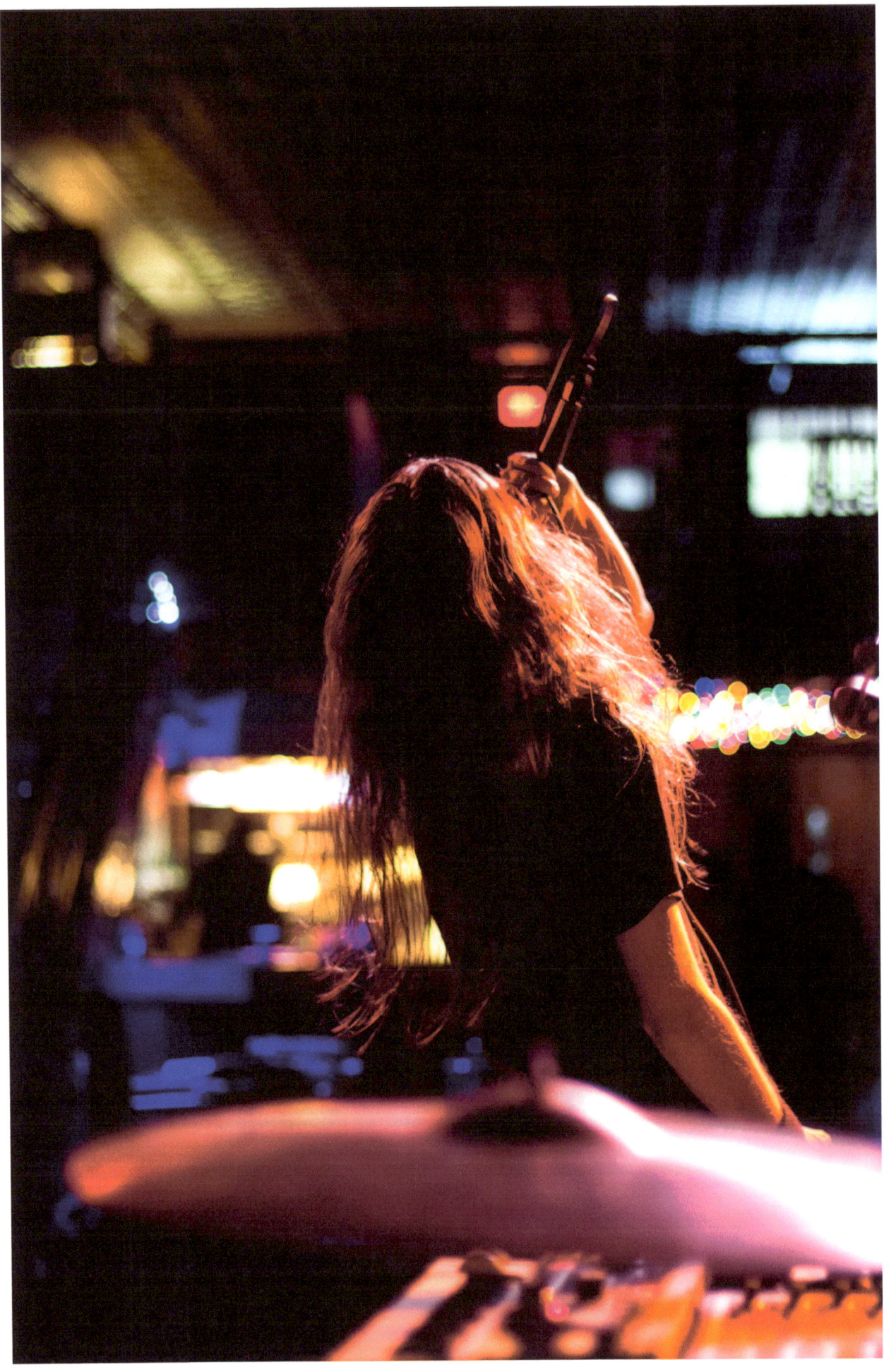

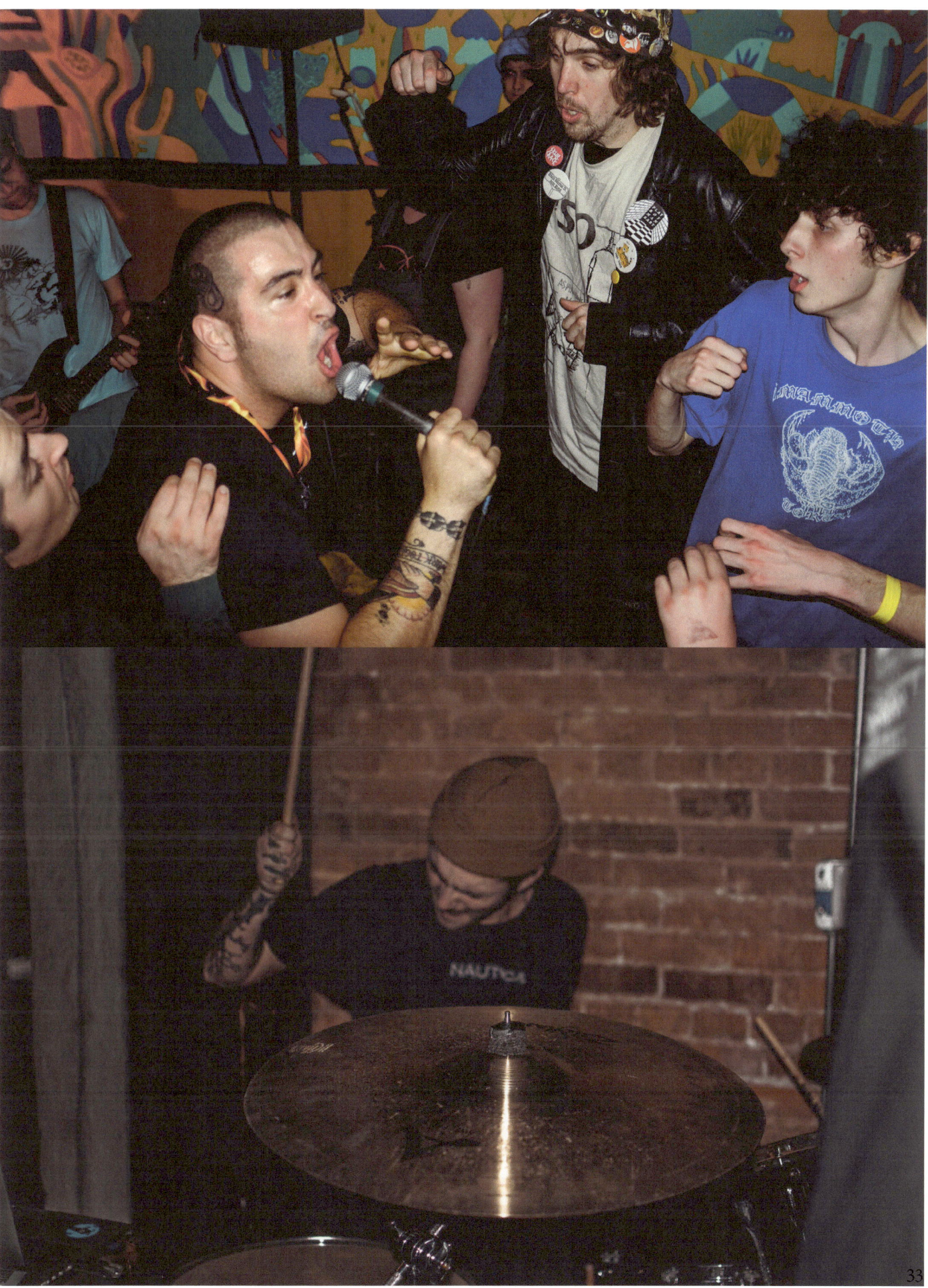

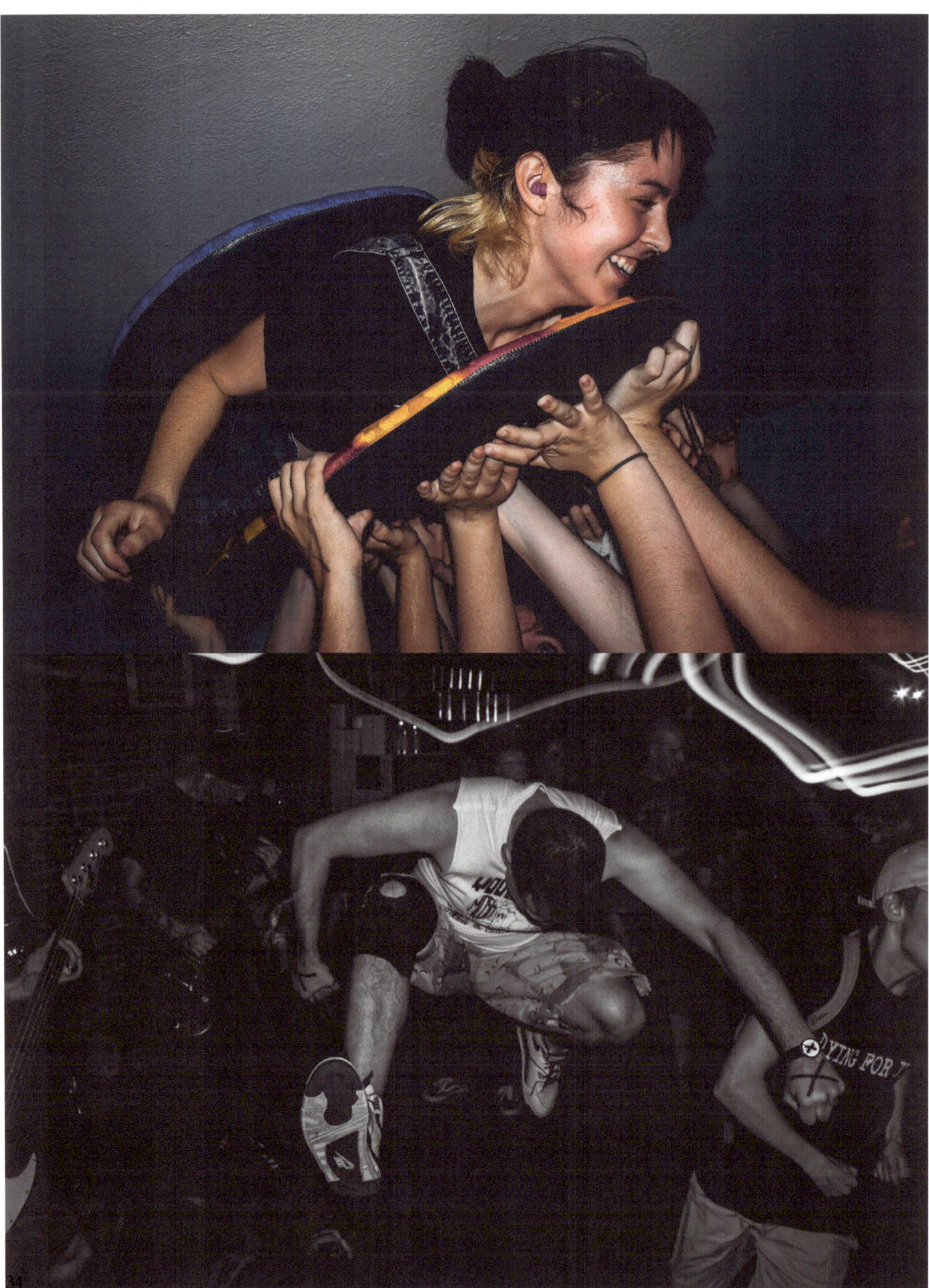

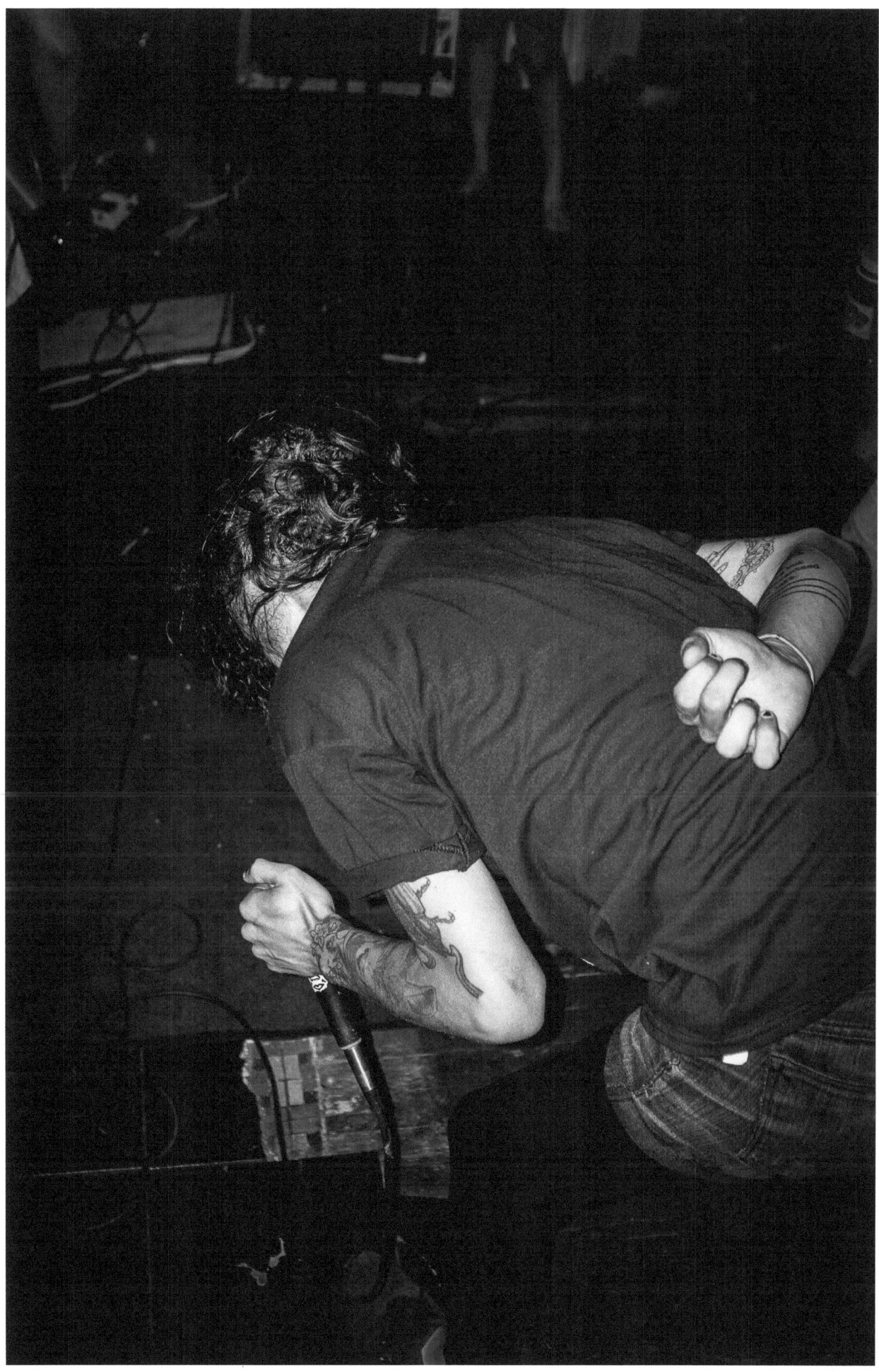

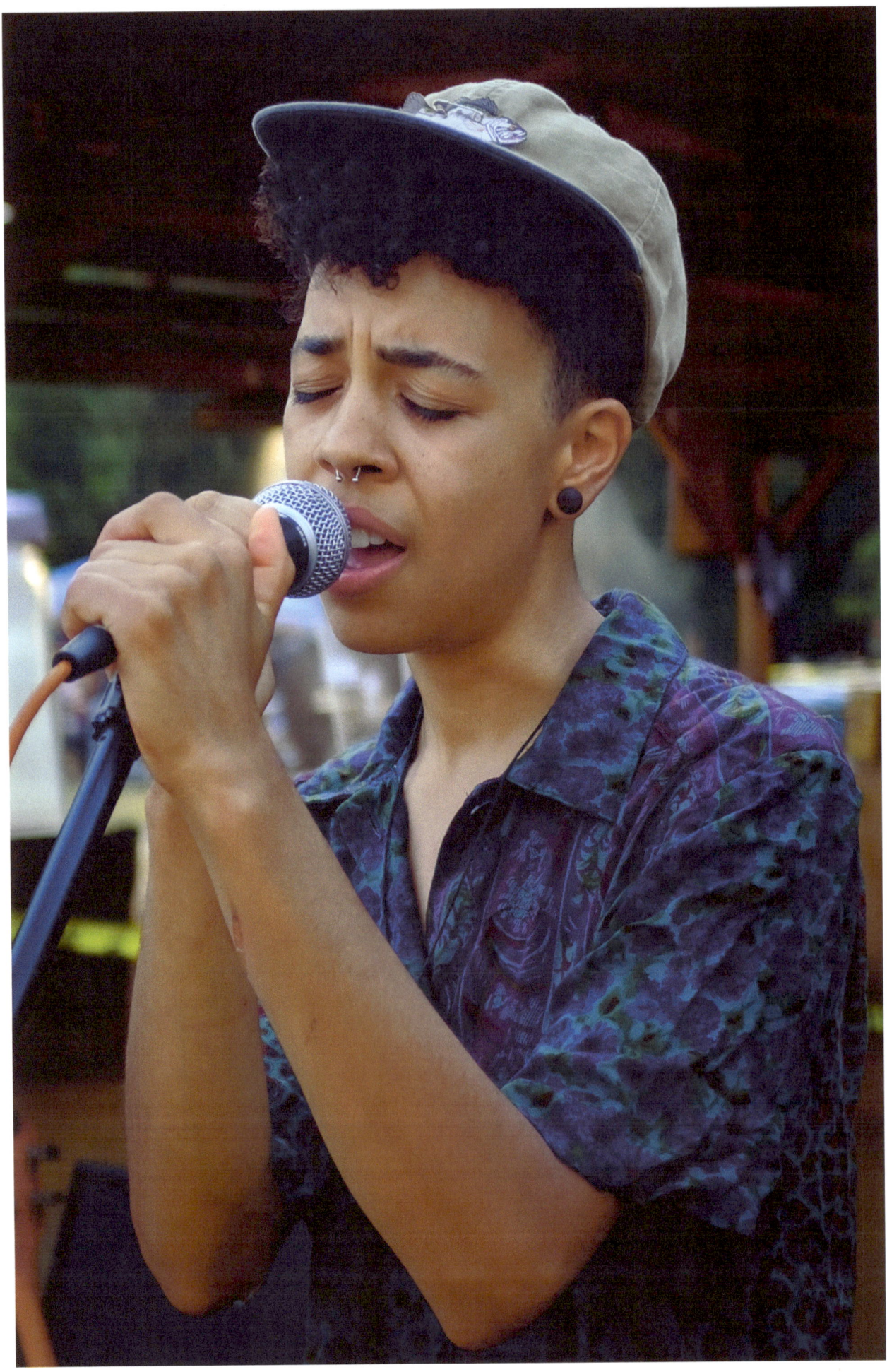

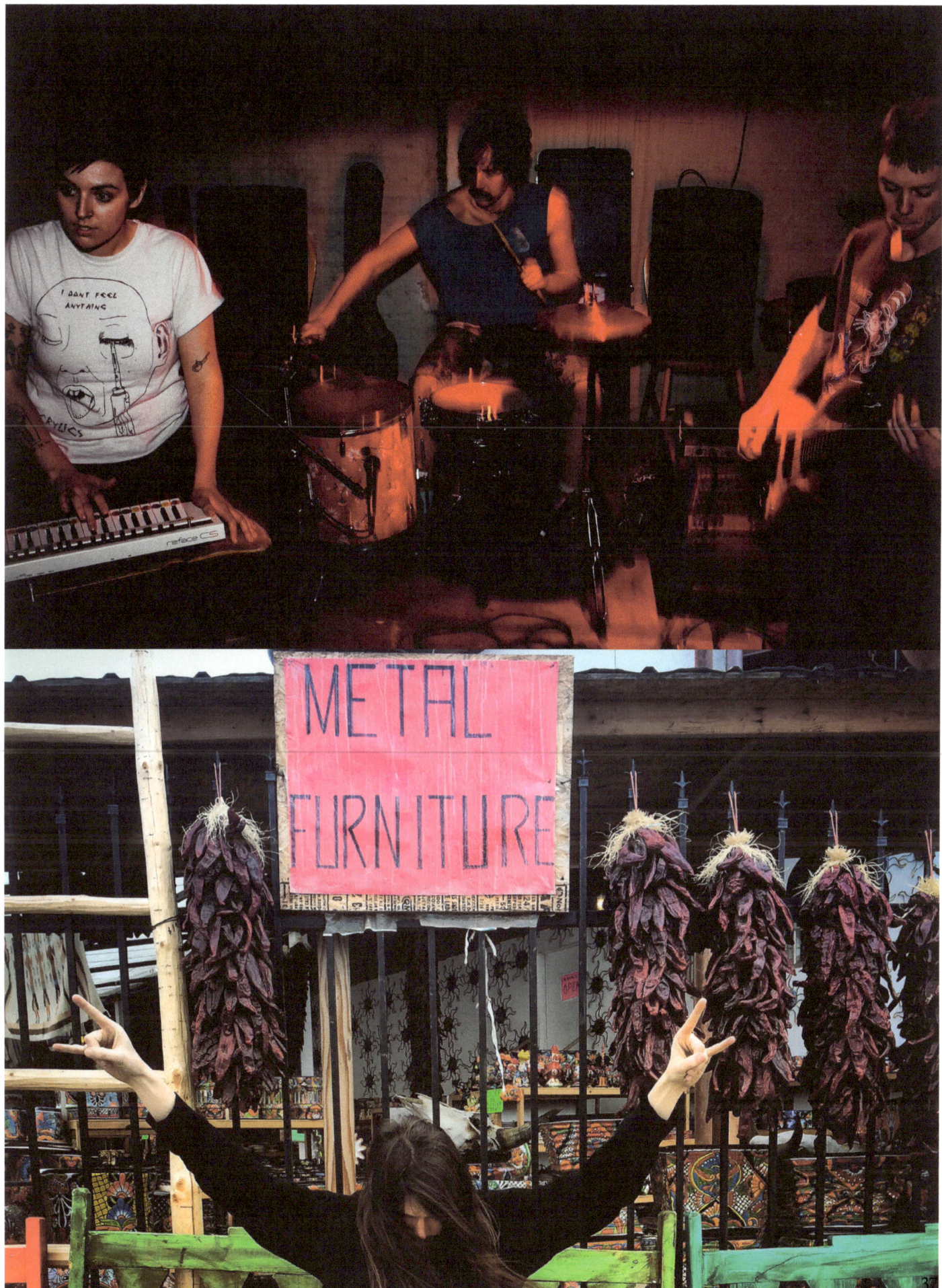

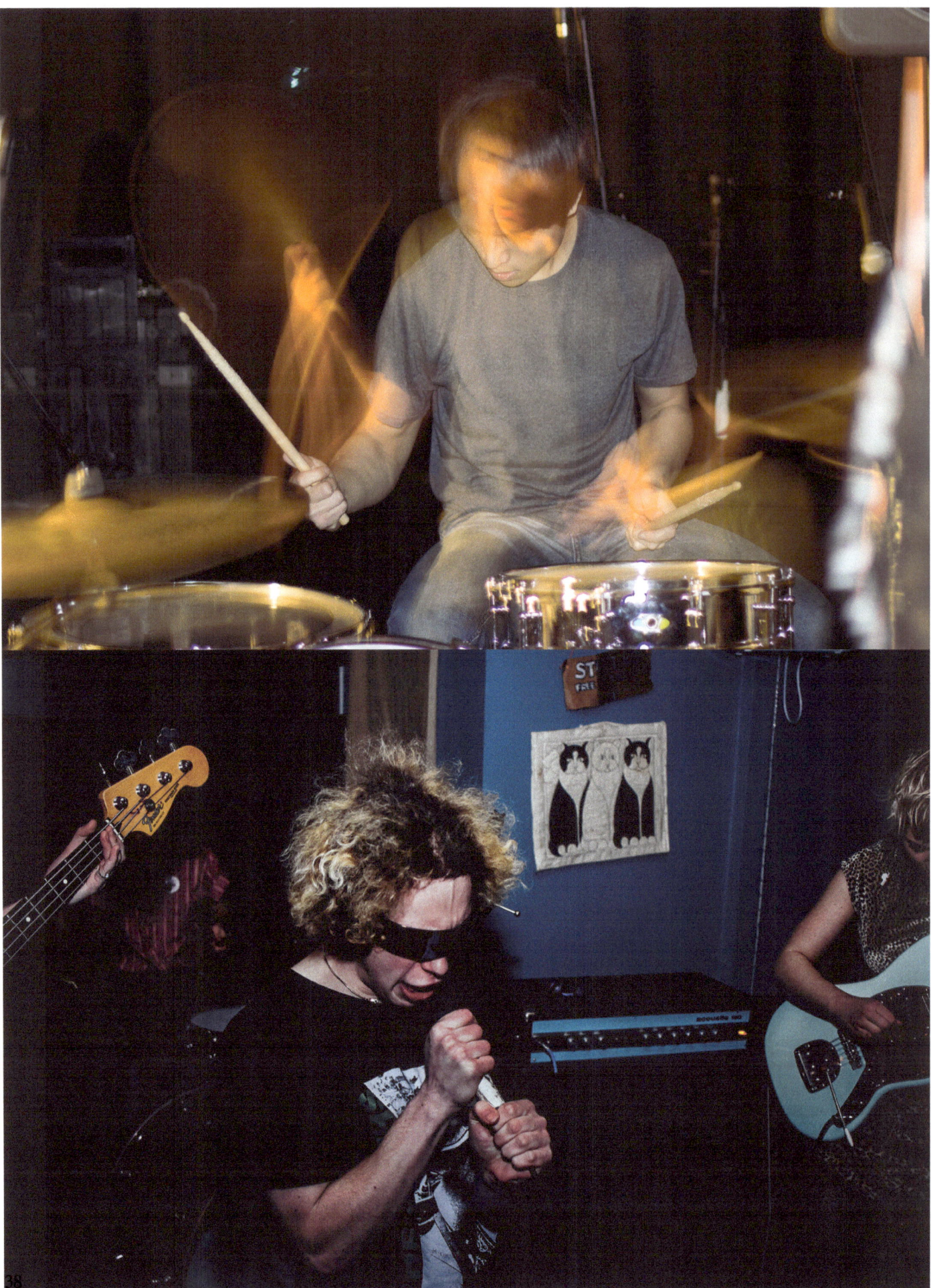

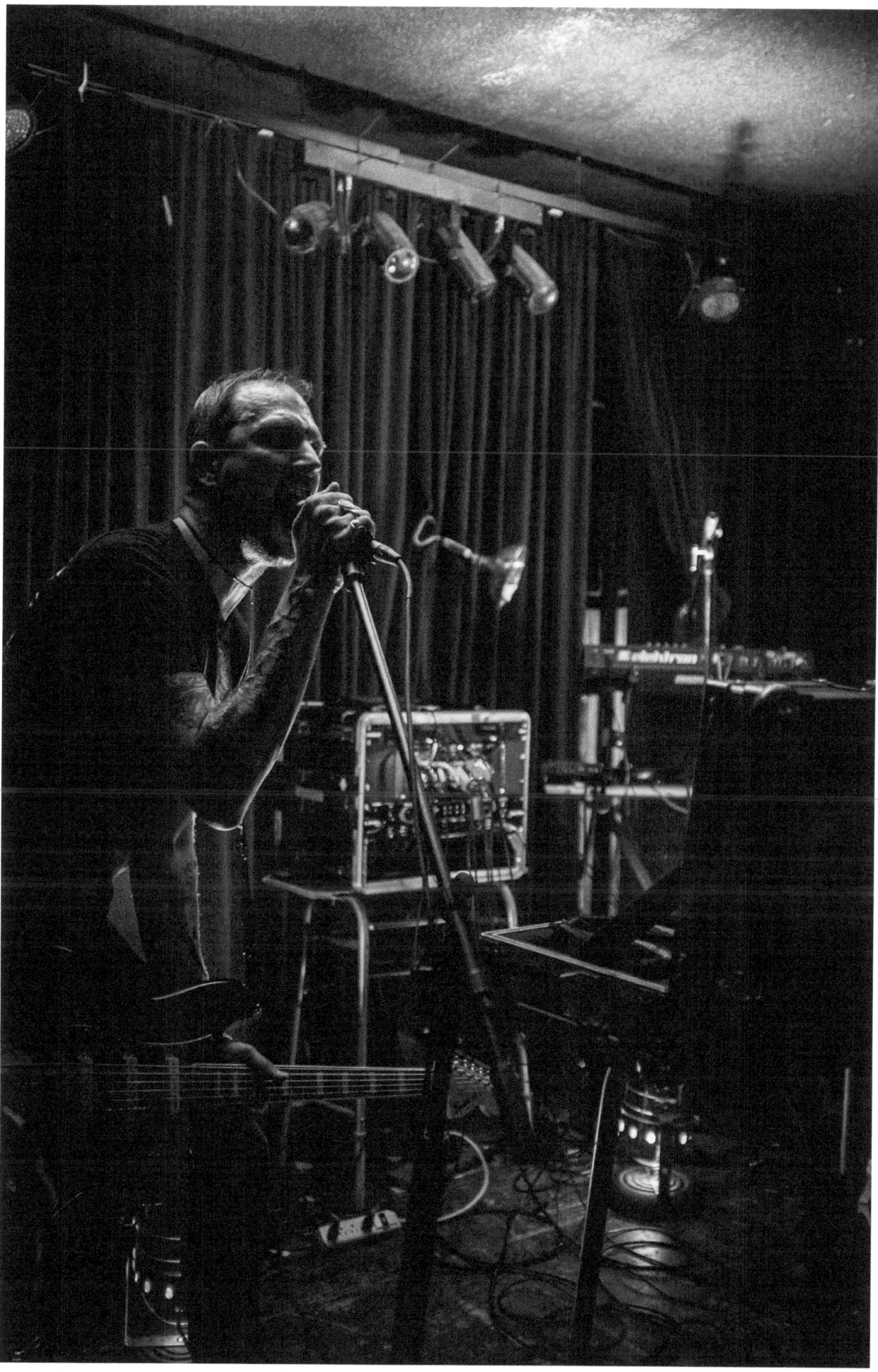

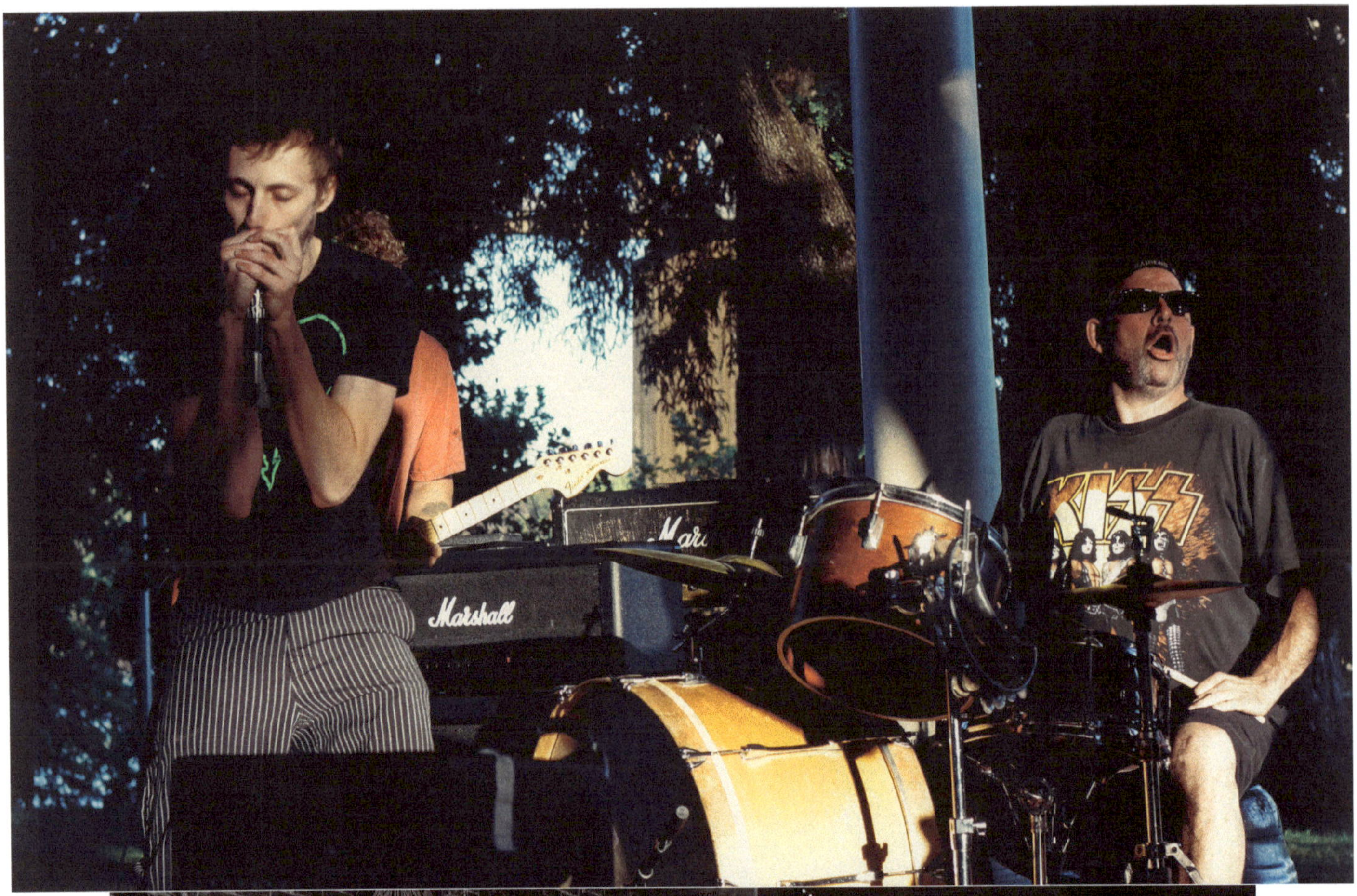

40

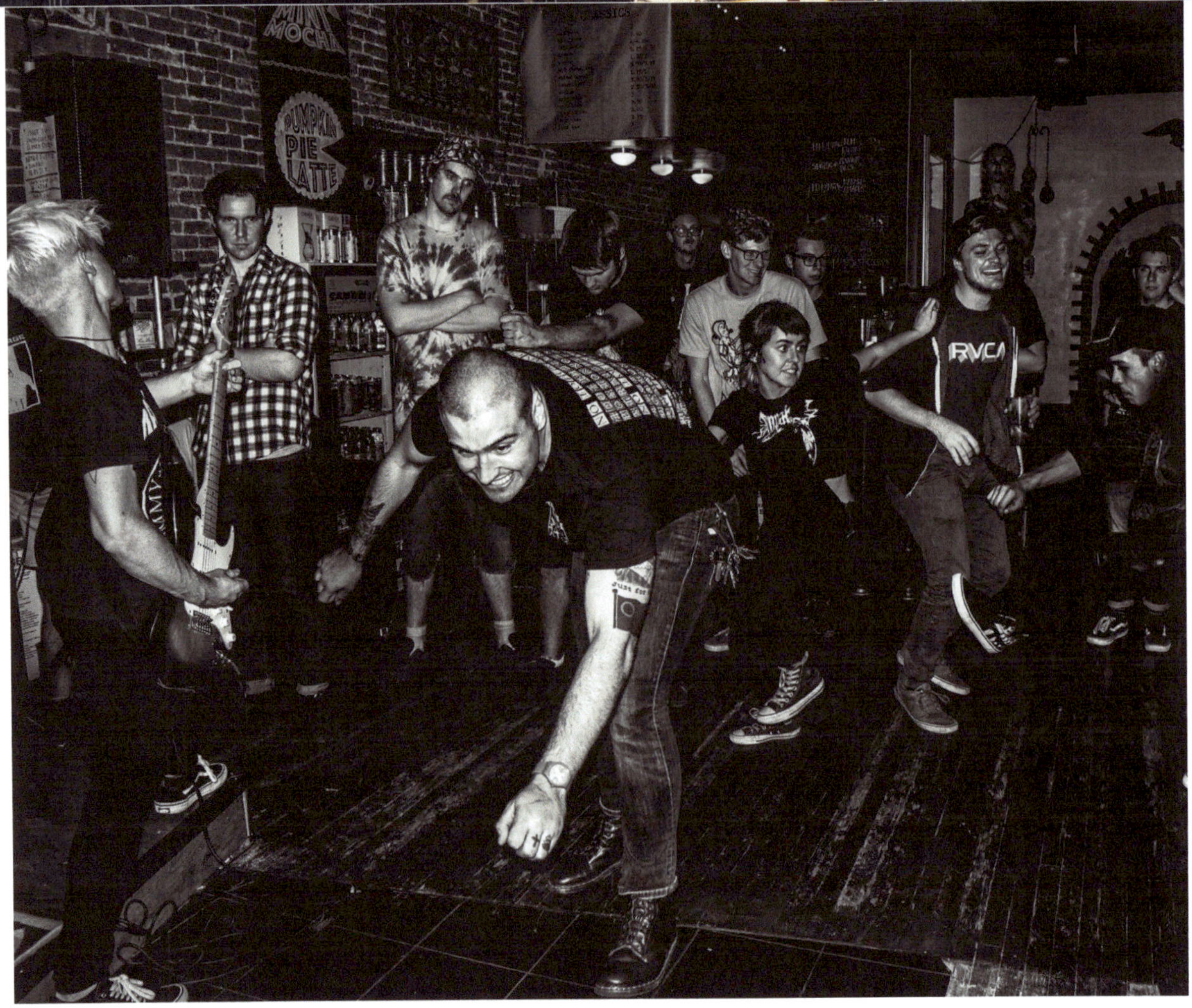

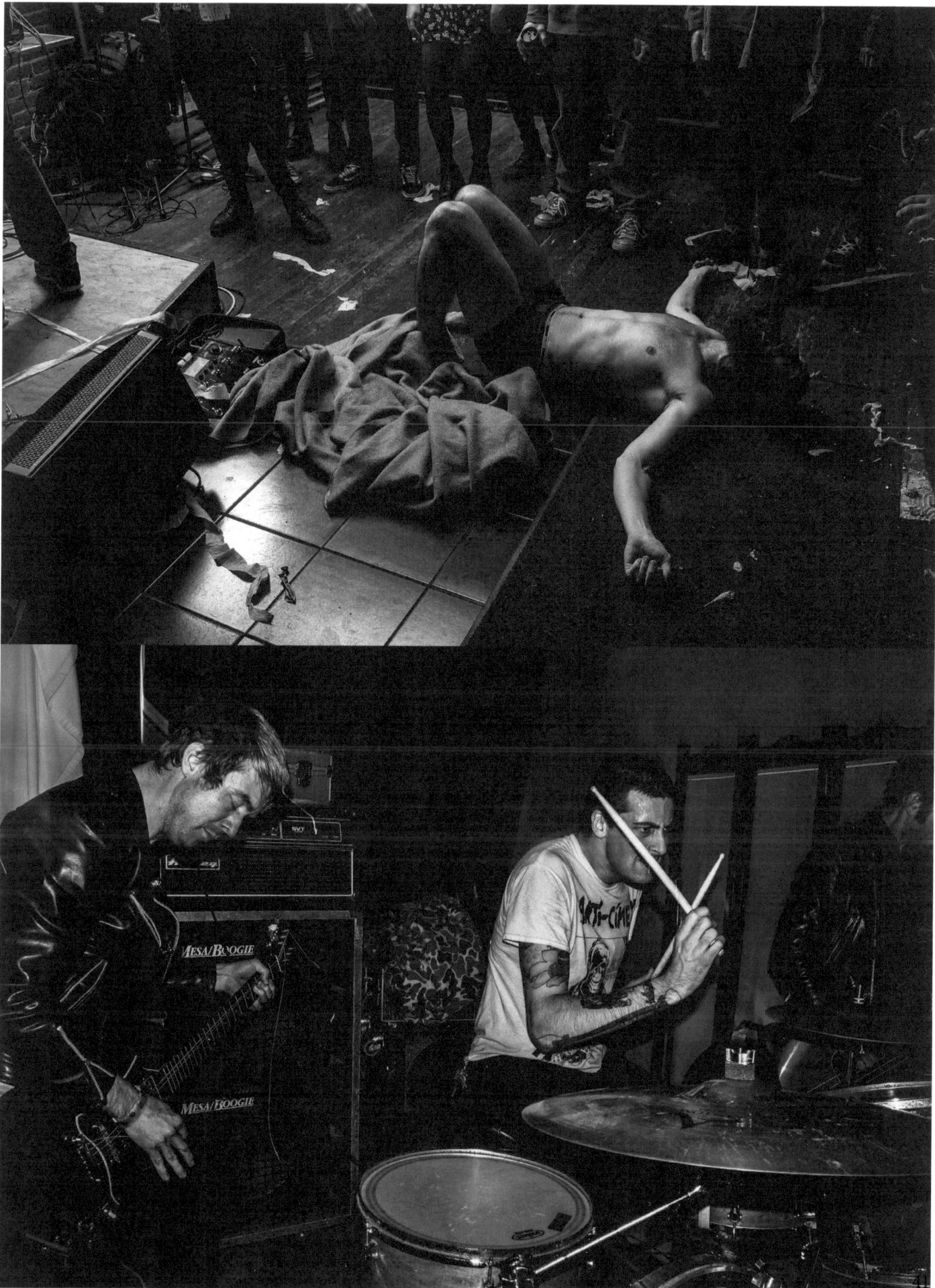

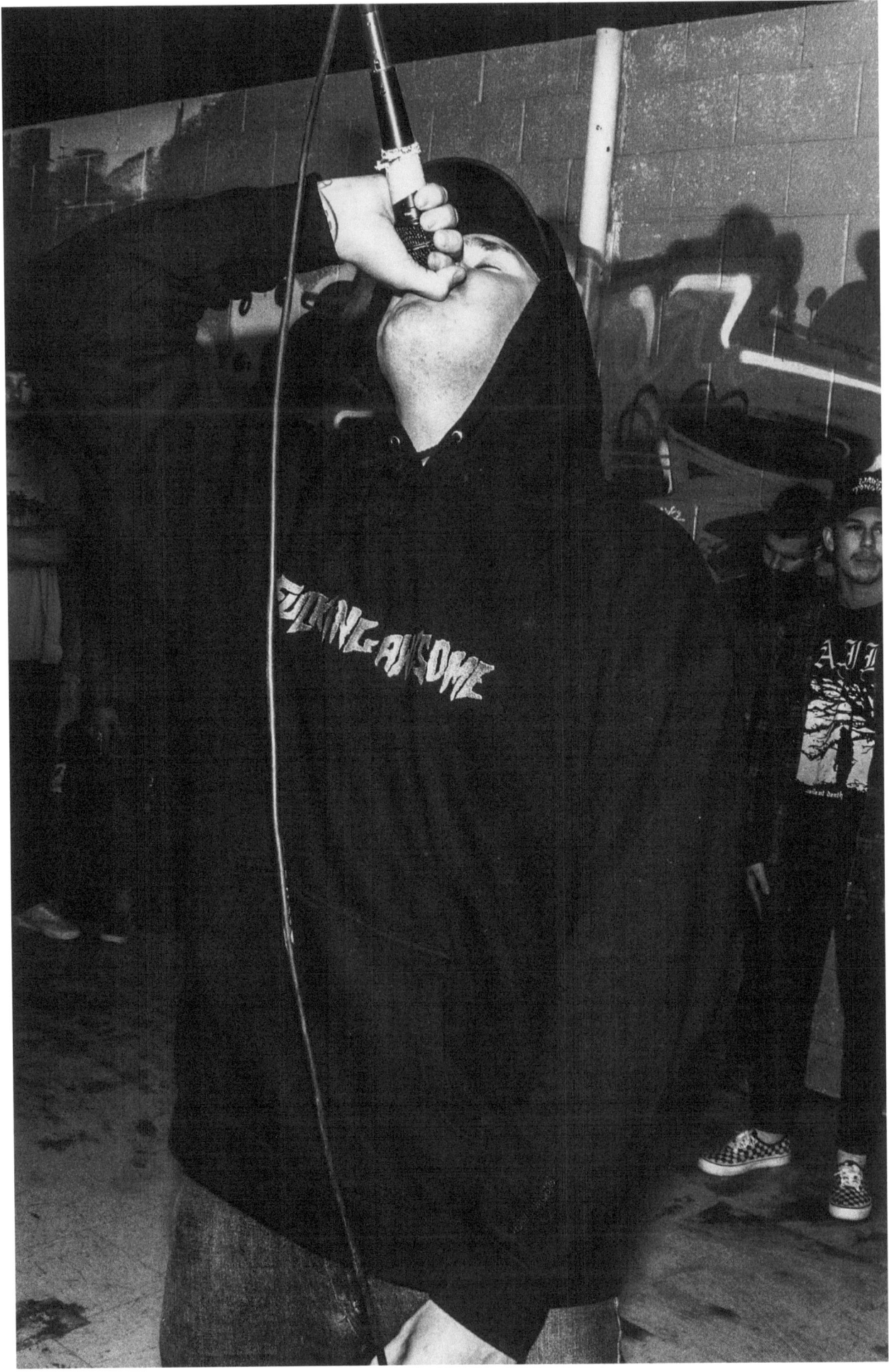

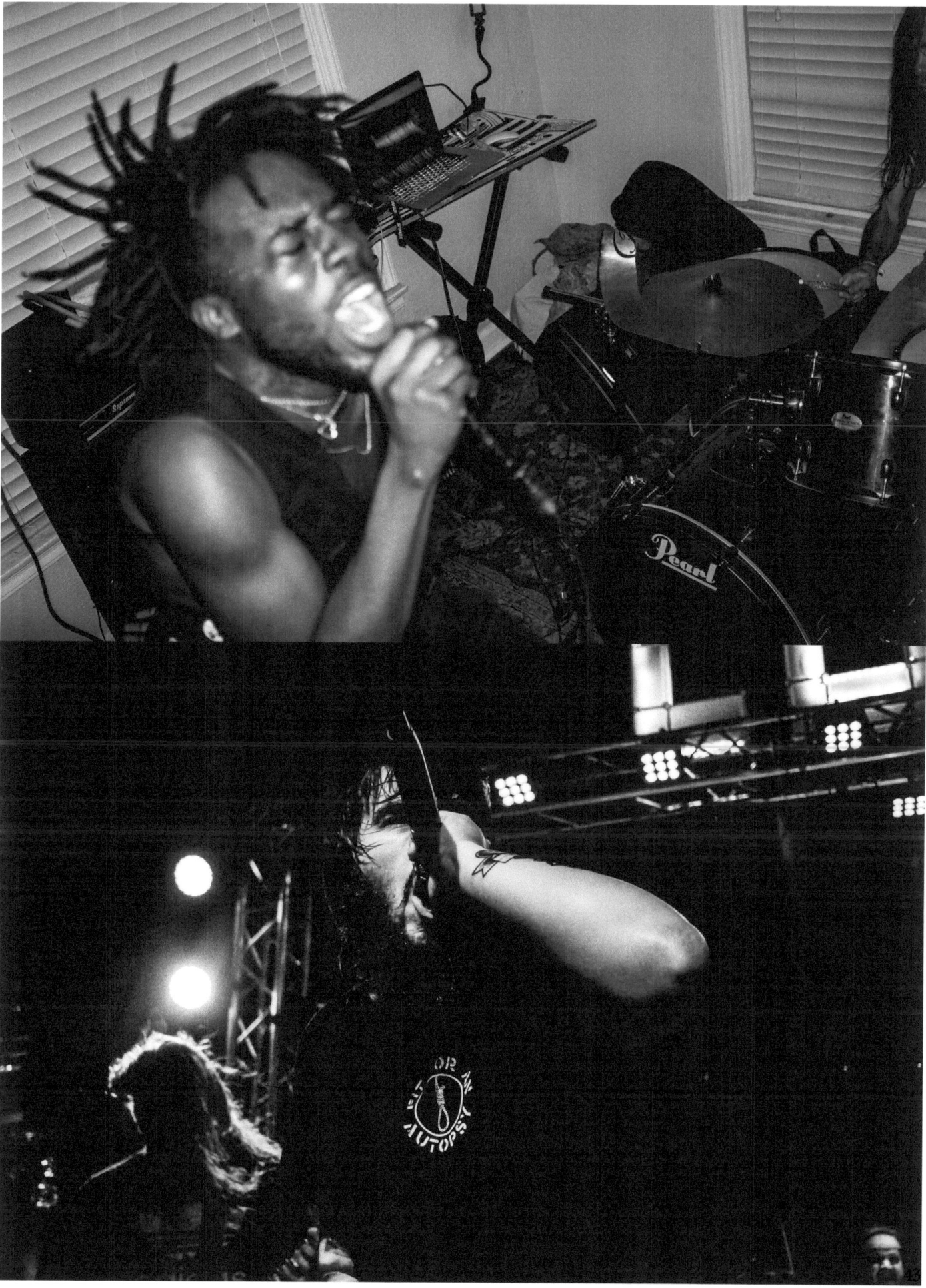

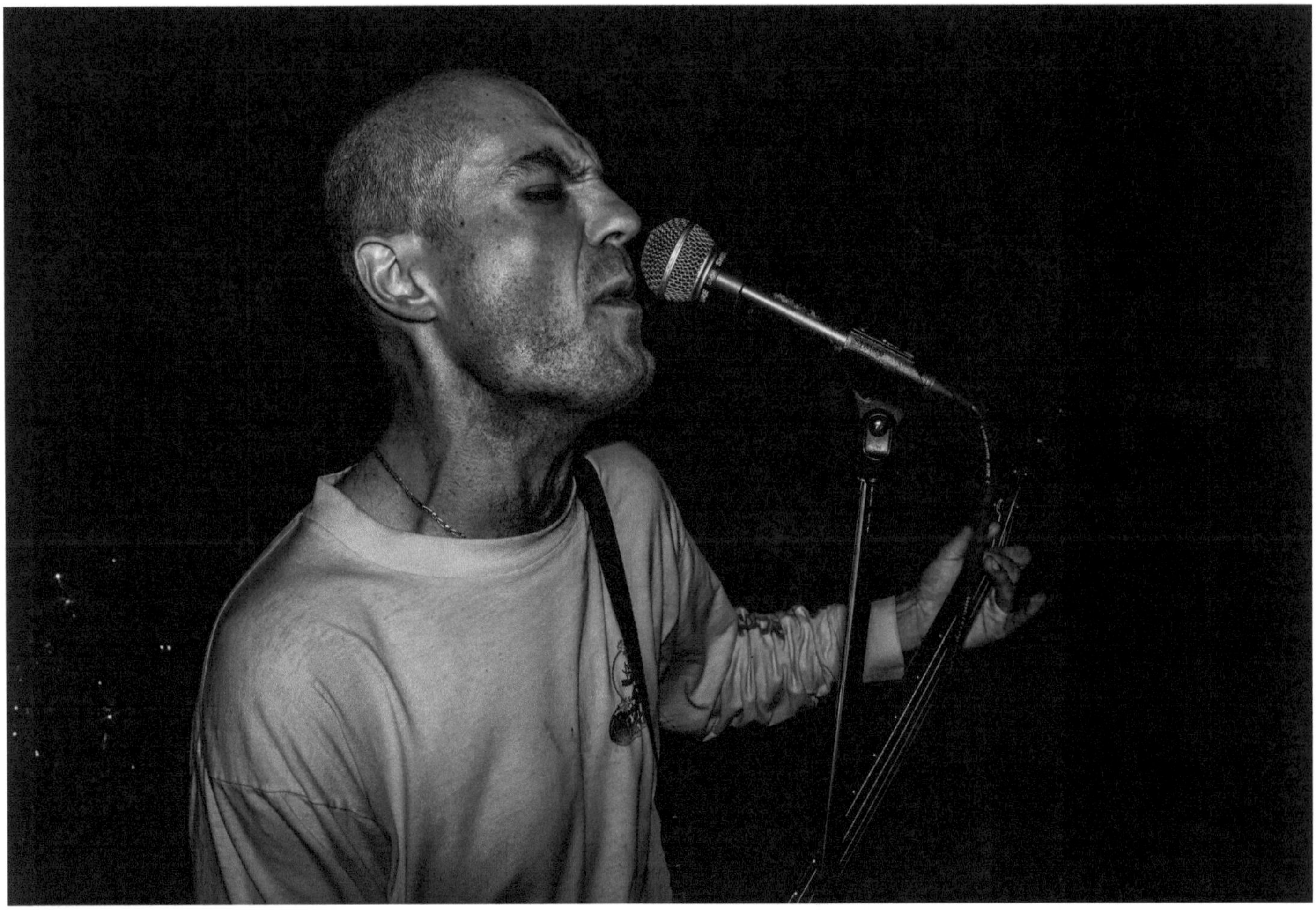

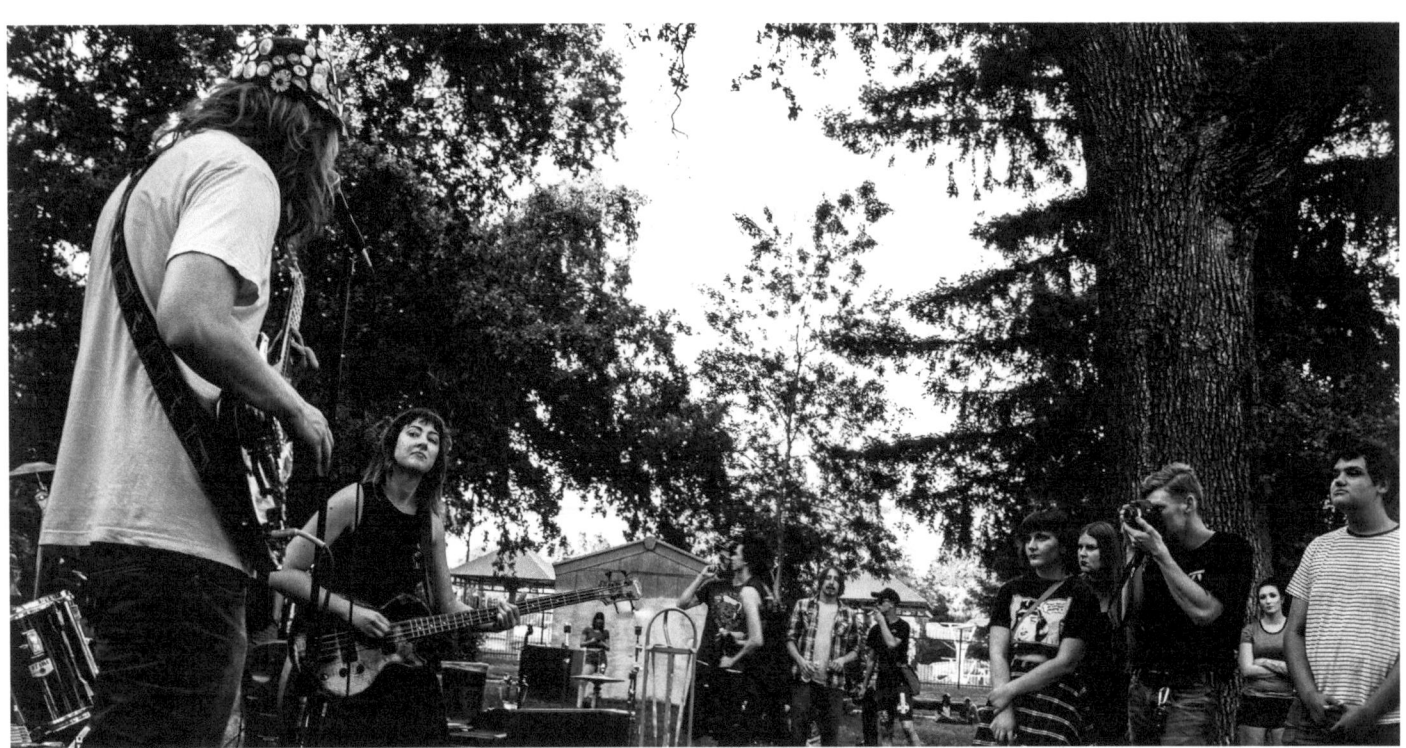

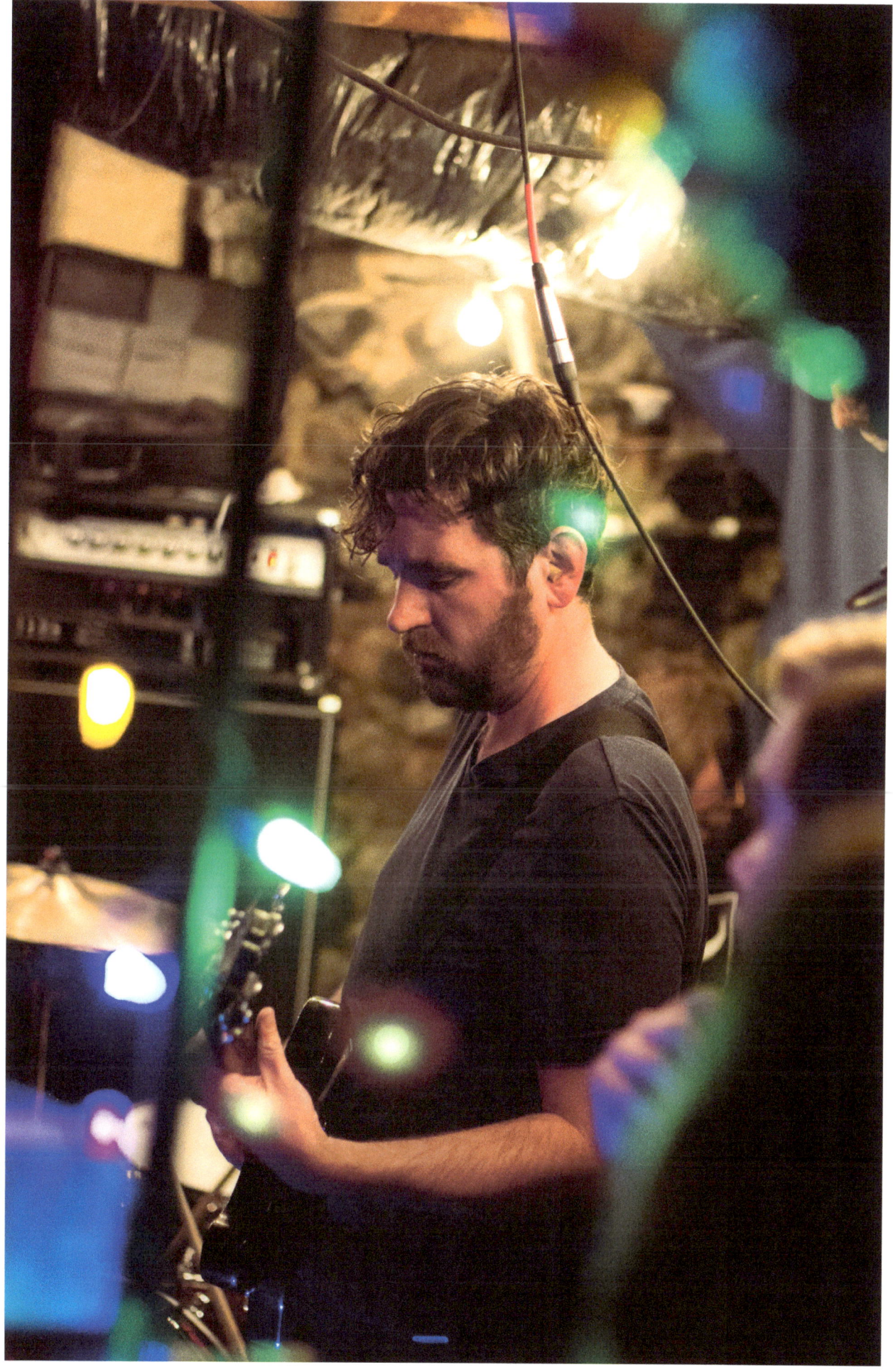

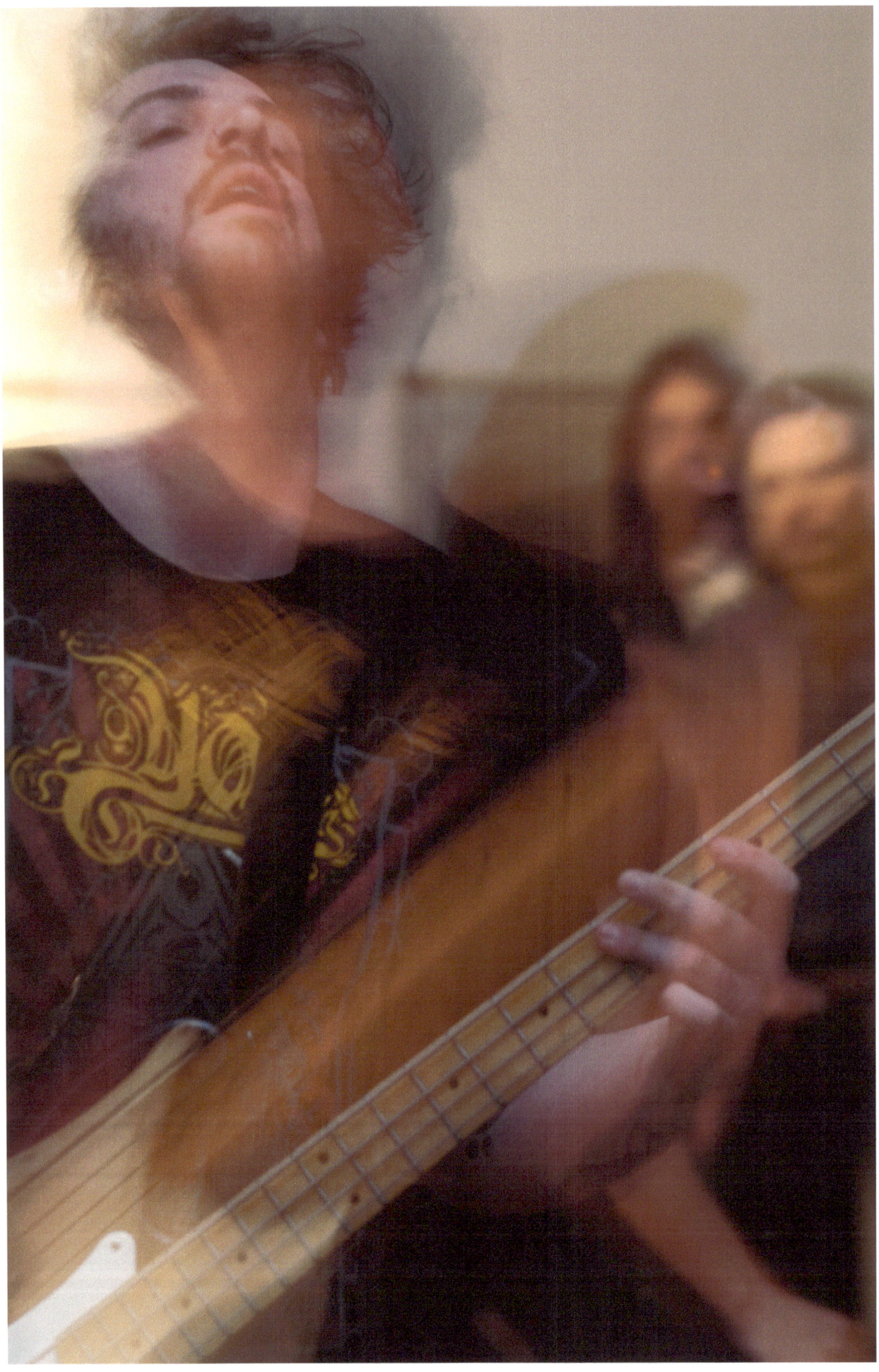

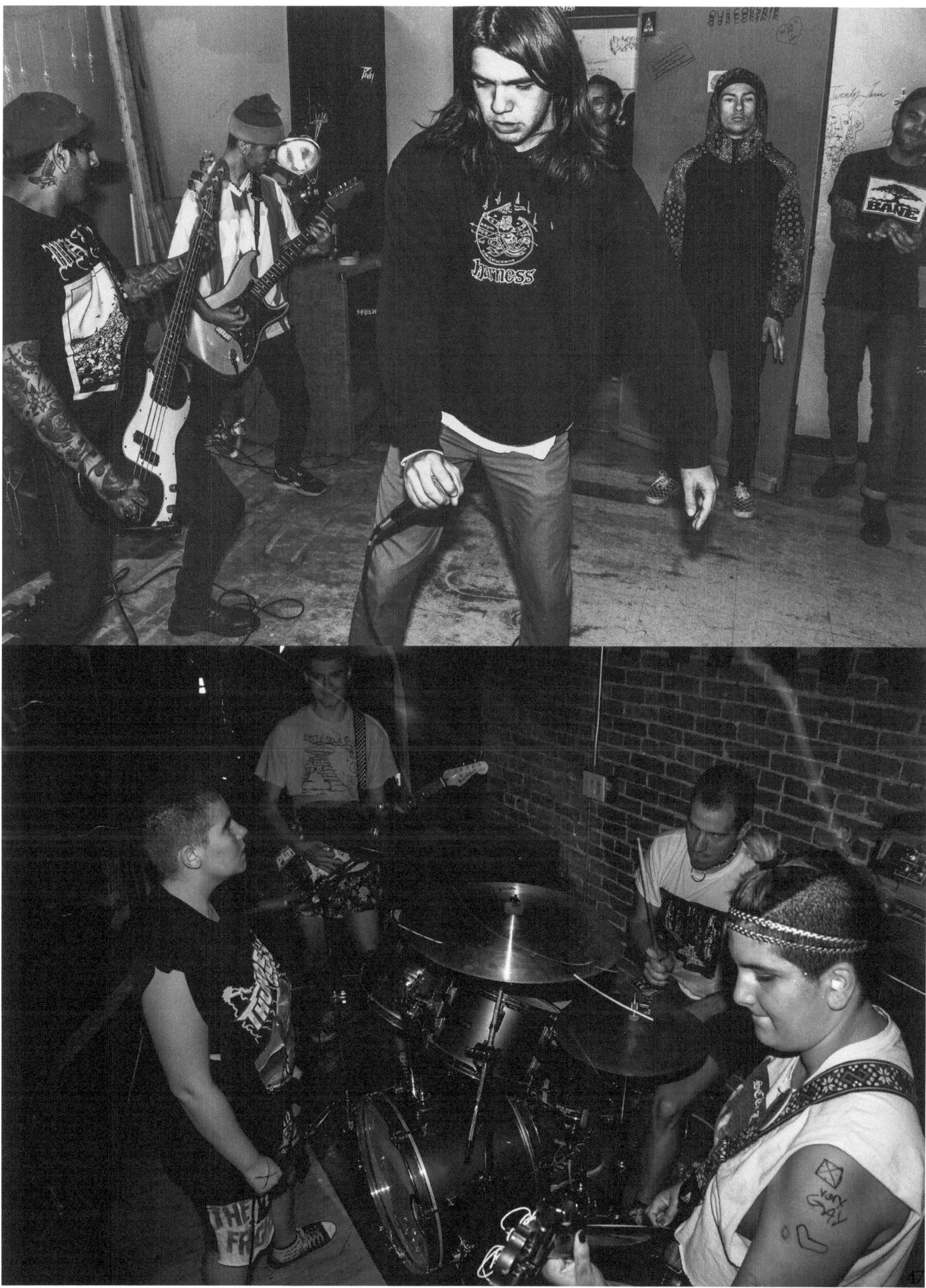

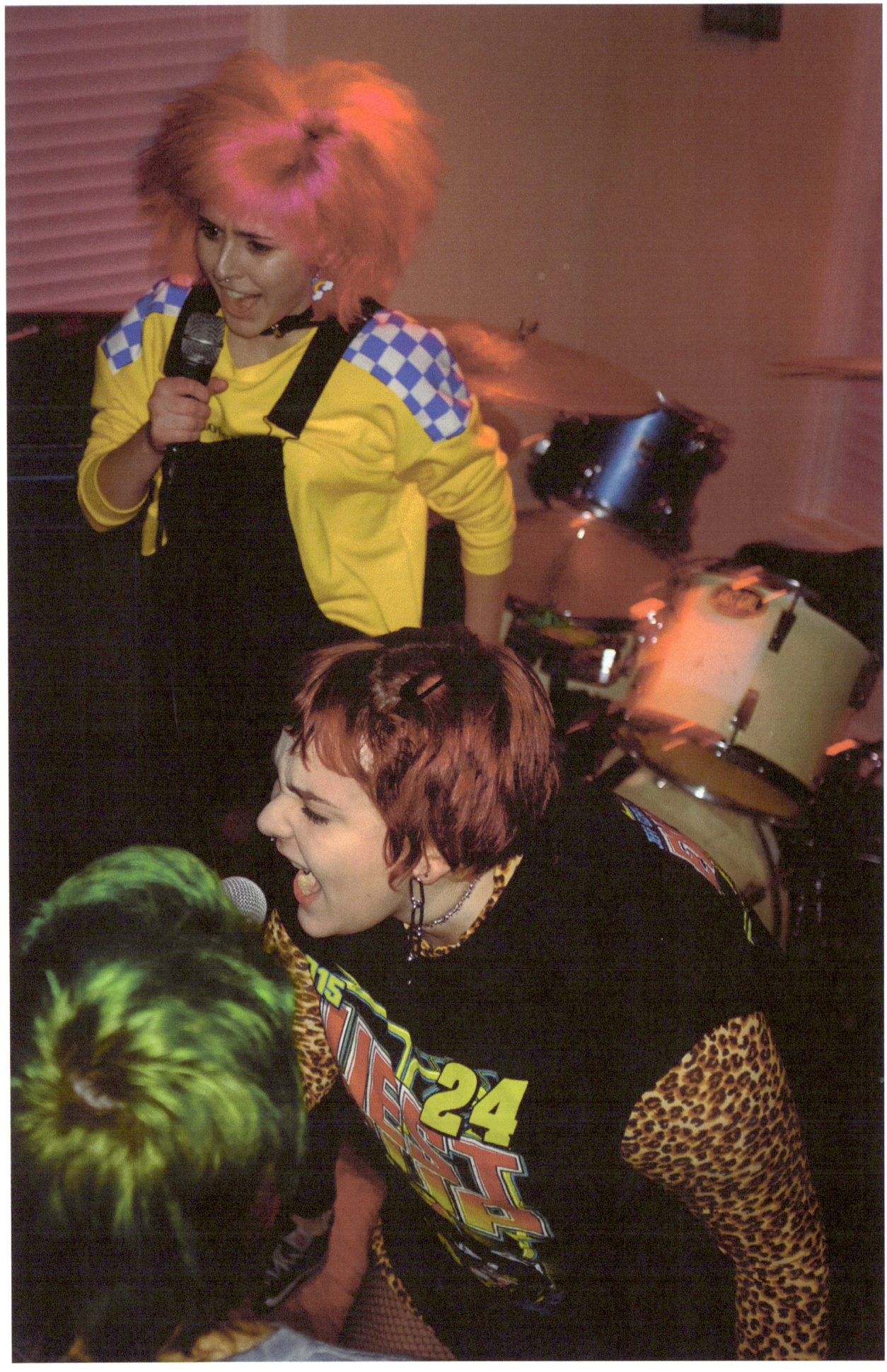

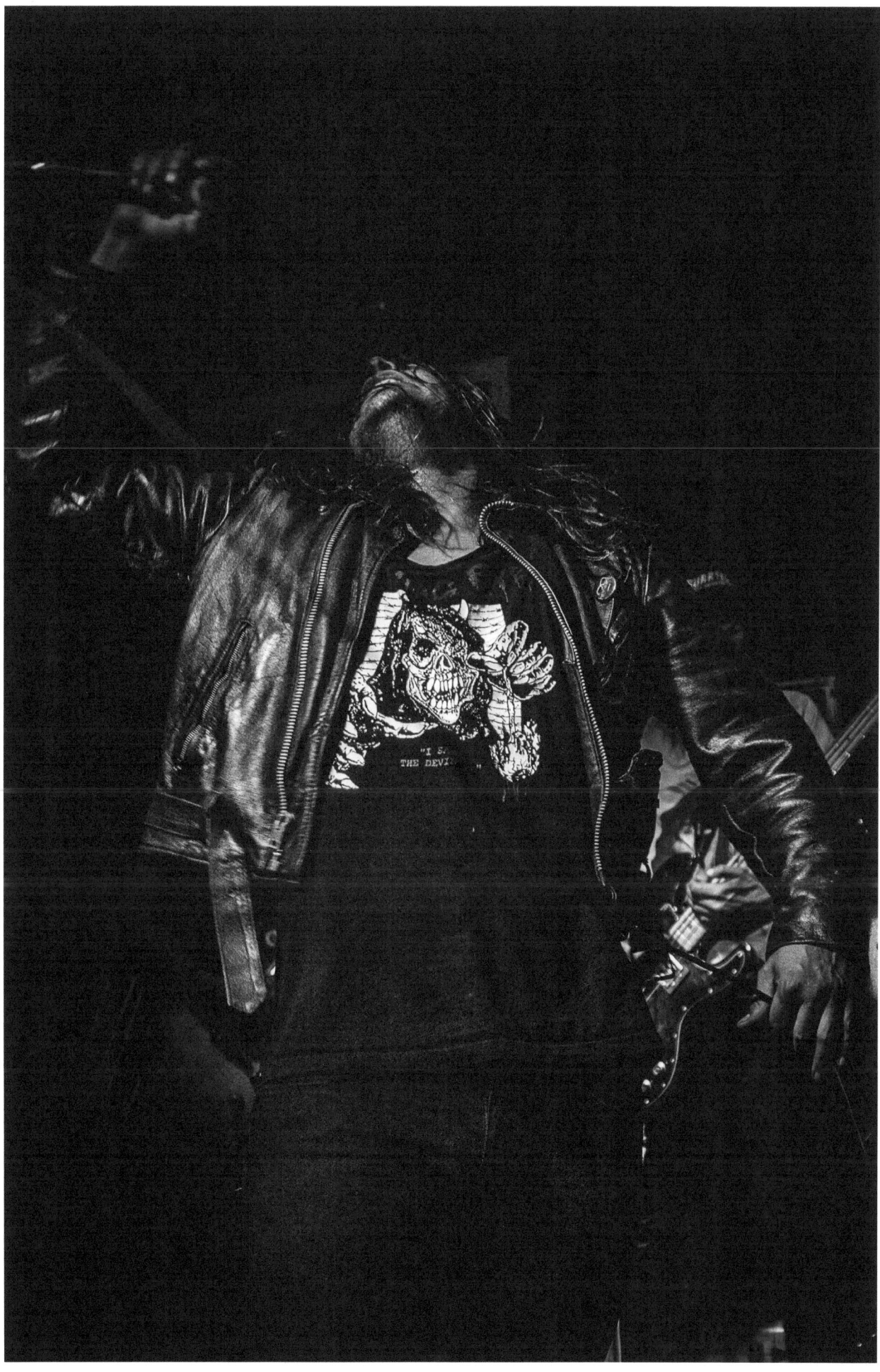

CREDITS

P4 - Pervert @ Raw Haus (Chico CA) by Bryan Hannah

P4 - The Convictions @ Naked Lounge (Chico CA) by Travis California

P5 - Not Shit @ Bridgetown DIY (La Puente CA) - Miles Claibourn

P6 - Brandon Squyres with Amarok @ 1078 Gallery (Chico CA) by Michelle Camy

P7 - Endon @ Cafe Coda (Chico CA) by John Simcox

P8 - The Surge @ CYC (Fresno CA) by Sean Mellon

P8 - Sapien @ Monstros Pizza for Kylee's memorial (Chico CA) by Khari Cowell

P9 - Minority Whip @ Naked Lounge (Chico CA) by Miles Claibourn

P9 - Cell Block @ Monstros Pizza (Chico CA) by Sean Mellon

P10 - Barefoot musician, walking coast to coast with cat. Near Los Osos, CA. February 2015. by Michelle Camy

P11 - FLQ @ Naked Lounge (Chico CA) by Miles Claibourn

P11 - Cell Block as Bikini Kill for Halloween (Chico CA) by Travis California

P12 - Outside Looking In @ Raw Haus (Chico CA) by Khari Cowell

P12 - Ghost Town Atlas @ The Temple (Redding CA) Sean Mellon

P13 - Endon @ Cafe Coda (Chico CA) by John Simcox

P14 - Hyde Park @ The Underground (Salt Lake City UT) by Sean Mellon

P14 - The Convictions @ Naked Lounge (Chico CA) by Travis California

P15 - Pervert @ Maltese (Chico CA) by John Simcox

P16 - Amarok @ Raw Haus (Chico CA) by Bryan Hannah

P16 - Mass Arrest @ Lucky Duck Bike Cafe (Oakland CA) by Miles Claibourn

P17 - Surrogate (Chico CA) by Michelle Camy

P17 - Pervert (Chico CA) by Khari Cowell

P18 - Amarok @ Cafe Coda by Michelle Camy

P19 - Beta Boys @ Chum Bucket (Chico CA) by Bryan Hannah

P19 - Dying For It @ The Colony (Sacramento CA) by Sean Mellon

P20 - NO! (Kevin Von Mutant) in Oakland CA. Anti-Capitalist Industrial Music by John Simcox

P21 - Cold Blue Mountain. July 2012. Horses provided by Roche's Training Stables, Chico, CA. by Michelle Camy

P21 - Crowd at The Colonny (Sacramento CA) by Miles Claibourn

P22 - Drain @ The Underground (SLC, UT) by Sean Mellon

P22 - Newlyweds in Seattle WA by Khari Cowell

P23 - Jake Hollingsworth of Heated @ Naked Lounge (Chico CA) by John Simcox

P23 - Control Test @ Chum Bucket by Bryan Hannah

P24 - Outside Looking In @ Monstros Pizza for Kylee's memorial (Chico CA) by Khari Cowell

P24 - Hounds @ Raw Haus (Chico CA) by Travis California

P25 - Sebass getting loose @ Naked Lounge (Chico CA) by Miles Claibourn

P25 - "Relaxing at a Show" @ Monstros Pizza (Chico CA) by Michelle Camy

P26 - Daniel Taylor, Esq; on tour with Cold Blue Mountain 2015 by Michelle Camy

P27 - Jonathan Richman 11/29/17 @ Blackbird Cafe (Chico CA) by Travis California

P27 - Monarch @ Cade Coda by Sean Mellon

P28 - Decline @ Naked Lounge (Chico CA) by John Simcox

P28 - The Cux @ Chum Bucket (Chico CA) by Bryan Hannah

P29 - Escuela 1/15/18 Raw Haus (Chico CA) by Travis California

P30 - Convictions @ Naked Lounge by Bryan Hannah

P30 - Drain @ The Underground (SLC, UT) by Sean Mellon

P31 - Cold Blue Mountain in Omaha, Nebraska (2015) by Michelle Camy

P31 - Decline @ Naked Lounge (Chico CA) by Bryan Hannah

P32 - Brandon Squyres. Des Moines, Iowa by Michelle Camy

P33 - Criminal Wave @ Naked Lounge (Chico CA) by Travis California

P33 - After Hours @ Naked Lounge (Chico CA) by Bryan Hannah

P34 - Crowd surfing to Drain @ Raw Haus by Bryan Hannah

P34 - Decline @ Naked Lounge (Chico CA) by Miles Claibourn

P35 - Connie Scarbossa of See You Space Cowboy…@ Naked Lounge (Chico CA)

P36 - Scout 9/3/17 @ Butcher Shop Theater (Chico CA) by Travis California

P37 - The Hecks @ Rock n Roll Club House (Portland OR) by Khari Cowell

P37 - "Metal Furniture" Cold Blue Mountain on Tour, New Mexico by Michelle Camy

P38 - Wander in San Fransisco CA 2015 by Michelle Camy

P38 - Ziptie in Seattle WA by Khari Cowell

P39 - Echo Beds in Oakland CA by John Simcox

P40 - Hefner Wolfe @ Caldwell Park (Redding CA) by Khari Cowell

P40 - Crowd to Dying For It @ Naked Lounge (Chico CA) by Bryan Hannah

P41 - Steaksauce Mustache @ Naked Lounge (Chico CA) by John Simcox

P41 - Machine Gun @ Honey Hive (SF CA) by Miles Claibourn

P42 - Liar's Tongue @ The Underground (SLC, UT) by Sean Mellon

P43 - Supplement 1/6/18 @ Raw Haus (Chico CA) by Travis California

P43 - Aberrance @ Lost On Main (Chico CA) by Khari Cowell

P44 - World Peace @ Honey Hive (SF CA) by Miles Claibourn

P44 - Central Valley Project @ Caldwell Park by Khari Cowell

P45 - Chris Keene, on tour with Cold Blue Mountain, 2015. Spokane, WA by Michelle Camy

P46 - Adrian Hammons with Cold Blue Mountain. January 2013. Chico, CA by Michelle Camy

P47 - Resonate @ The Underground (SLC, UT) by Sean Mellon

P47 - Deadname @ Naked Lounge (Chico CA) by Miles Claibourn

P48 - Gay Boy Gang @ Raw Haus (Chico CA) by Miles Claibourn

P49 - Fantasy Lane @ Maltese (Chico CA) by John Simcox

www.ingramcontent.com/pod-product-compliance
Lightning Source LLC
Chambersburg PA
CBHW042322250526
R18347200002B/R183472PG45473CBX00010B/11